Listening to
Classic American
Popular Songs

ALLEN FORTE

Listening to Classic American Popular Songs

Vocal Interpretations by Richard Lalli,
with Pianist Gary Chapman

YALE UNIVERSITY PRESS   NEW HAVEN AND LONDON

Designed by Sonia Shannon
Set in Electra type by Tseng Information Systems, Inc.
Printed in the United States of America by
R. R. Donnelley & Sons, Harrisonburg, Virginia.

Library of Congress Cataloging-in-Publication Data
Forte, Allen.
Listening to classic American popular songs /
Allen Forte ; vocal interpretations by Richard Lalli,
with pianist Gary Chapman.
p.   cm.
Includes bibliographical references (p.) and index.
ISBN 0-300-08338-6
1. Popular music — United States — History and criticism.
I. Lalli, Richard, baritone.   II. Chapman, Gary.   III. Title.
ML3477 .F672   2001
782.42164′0973 — dc21
00-011309

A catalogue record for this book is available from the
British Library.

The paper in this book meets the guidelines
for permanence and durability of the Committee on
Production Guidelines for Book Longevity of
the Council on Library Resources.

10 9 8 7 6 5 4 3 2 1

To Madeleine

The publication of this book
would not be possible without the generous support
of Susanne Scherer Klingeman and
Henry S. Scherer, Jr., '53,
in memory of their father, Henry S. Scherer,
who loved Yale and
American popular music.

Further, the publishers gratefully acknowledge
the Kay Swift Memorial Trust
for a significant contribution toward
the successful completion of this project.

Contents

Preface

This book introduces the reader to the classic American popular song, that wonderful repertoire of music composed from about 1925 to about 1950 that many regard as the golden era of vernacular American music. These magical songs have spoken to generations of Americans and to people all over the world in a musical language of love, hope, whimsical humor, irony, and, sometimes, despair. To experience these songs is to partake of the glamour and splendid artificiality of Broadway and Hollywood in the period that begins after World War I, extends through the Great Depression, World War II, and ends in the relatively peaceful and happy time of postwar America.

The special status of popular song during the second quarter of this century is due to a number of factors, among them the flourishing development of American musical theater and, later, the movie musical, the advent of radio and the proliferation of recorded music. Deeper and more elusive reasons are to be found in the music itself and in the remarkable creative qualities songwriters brought to what in other periods might well be described as ephemeral music.

It was during this period, especially its early stages, that a number of salutary influences coalesced to form the creative matrix out of which the repertoire took shape. Among these are the influence of jazz, which, with its African-American origins, played a central role in the formation of a truly American idiom. There are of course other important features, many of which can be traced back to European sources but which were bent considerably out of shape by such inventive musical minds as those of Jerome Kern, Irving Berlin, Cole Porter, George Gershwin, Richard Rodgers, Harold Arlen, and a host of other extraordinarily talented, but perhaps not as well known, songwriters of the era.

Coextensive with the purely musical development of this period was the emergence of talented lyricists: Ted Koehler, Howard Dietz, Edward Eliscu, Ira Gershwin, Lorenz Hart, E. Y. Harburg, Oscar Hammerstein II, Dorothy Fields, Johnny Mercer, Johnny Burke, and others, not to ignore Irving Berlin and Cole Porter, who were their own lyricists. With the passing of these remarkably talented individuals, only a few special persons, for instance, Jimmy Van Heusen, were waiting in the wings to replace them. Thus, the enormous productivity of the golden era petered out, ending around 1950, and leaving the unique repertoire of song that is the subject of this book.[1]

The book focuses on selected individual songs within this very large repertoire, on their special qualities, and on the ways in which the music and words
of each song interact to create unique and expressive music, music to which listeners may respond with varying degrees of emotional intensity. It is the remarkable characteristics of these songs that have kept them alive and popular over
many years and that enable them to speak anew to each successive generation:
the beautiful melodies and harmonies, the entrancing rhythms, the wondrous
lyrics that are so often inseparably bonded to the musical notes in such extraordinary ways. These qualities, which evoke universal responses from sensitive listeners, inspired the use of the term "classic" to convey the timelessness of the
best of this music.

The book is for those who can read music and would like to know more about
this music and deepen their experience of it. It is not intended for professional
musicians, although of course they are welcome to read it as well. An introductory section prepares the reader for some of the very basic technical material, but
this review can be omitted by those who already have some elementary musical
knowledge. Everyone, however, may wish to read the sections on melody and
lyrics.

A special feature of the book is the inclusion of a compact disc that contains recorded performances of all the songs to be discussed (except "But Beautiful," for which the recording rights could not be negotiated). These interpretations have been specially prepared by baritone Richard Lalli and pianist Gary
Chapman, expert musicians who have had extensive experience performing this
unique music.

Since some readers may know of my scholarly work in more academic areas
of music, I should like to offer a word of explanation concerning my participation in the writing of this book and in the preparation of the compact disc. My
experience with the classic American popular song extends back to a misspent
childhood during which, in addition to subjecting me to a traditional training
in music, my mother made me play popular music and jazz on the piano. Subsequently I played that music professionally, before seeing the error of my ways
and entering the cloistered academic life. This project has enabled me to revisit
that earlier phase of my work in music and to apply my skills to the realization
of a book that I sincerely hope will bring pleasure and satisfaction to the reader.

The idea for this book and the accompanying compact disc came from Di-
rector John Ryden and Music Editor Harry Haskell of Yale University Press. I
should like to thank both gentlemen for setting the difficult task of writing a
book of this kind and express my heartfelt appreciation for the many hours of
anguished labor that ensued.

I am also grateful for the opportunity to collaborate with Messrs. Richard Lalli and Gary Chapman in the preparation of the compact disc and especially for allowing me to accompany Mr. Lalli on two of the songs. My mother would be proud.

Many friends have expressed interest in this project, and I thank them all enthusiastically — especially Ron Williams, Clem Fucci, Mel Cooper, Edward De-Louise, Robert Gill, Andrew Graham, Mark Shoemaker, Barzillai Cheskis, and my dear friend Harold Switkes, who always does and says just the right thing. I am most grateful to my son Olen, who provided help and warm encouragement, and to my lovely wife, Madeleine, the dedicatee, whose support was indispensable.

Finally, I am enormously indebted to my friend and professional colleague Robert Aldridge for his many stimulating comments and for his invaluable recommendations, based upon a broad and deep experience with this repertoire of music.

Listening to
Classic American
Popular Songs

CHAPTER ONE

Preliminaries

The following brief review of some of the very basic technical material discussed in this book—melody, harmony, form, lyrics, rhythm—is meant to enhance the reader's understanding and, consequently, his or her enjoyment of the discussions of individual songs, particularly those who don't already possess some rudimentary musical knowledge beyond the ability to read music. I do recommend, however, that everyone read the sections on melody and lyrics.

MELODY

When we hear and see in music notation the topography of a particular melody, we can refer to the ordinary scale as a convenient and useful arrangement of notes, since it provides a specific way of locating the musical-spatial position of a note in a given key. Associated with these positions, called *scale degrees*, are consecutive numbers representing each note of the scale, as shown in Ex. 1-1.

1	2	3	4	5	6	7	8
Tonic				Dominant			

Ex. 1-1. Scale degrees

In addition to describing the position of a note within the scale by scale degree, traditional labels describe certain *functions* of notes in a key. For our purposes, only two such labels are necessary. Scale degree 1, called the *tonic* or *keynote*, functions as a centric pitch in the key, while scale degree 5 is called the *dominant*.[1]

The distance between adjacent notes of the scale varies between the smallest distance, called the *half step*, and the next larger distance (two half steps), called the *whole step*. On a piano keyboard scale degree 1 (Ex. 1-1) is separated from scale degree 2 by another key, the black key (F♯ or G♭). The distance between the two scale degrees is therefore a whole step. The same relation holds between all the adjacent scale degrees *except* scale degrees 3 and 4 and scale degrees 7 and 8, where there is no intervening key. Accordingly, those distances are half steps. Thus, the *major scale*, such as that represented in Ex. 1-1, consists of the following series of whole steps and half steps: whole-whole-half-whole-whole-whole-half. To use more precise terminology, the distance between any two notes, not just those that are adjacent, is called an *interval*. We will have occasion to use that term often in this book.

Before we introduce a few more terms and concepts, let us consider a portion of an actual melody, Stephen Foster's beautifully timeless encomium, "Jeannie With The Light Brown Hair."

As we listen to this melody (Ex. 1-2) we are probably aware of the simple

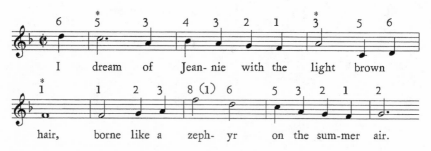

Ex. 1-2. *"I Dream of Jeannie"*

rhythms that emphasize certain notes by longer durations, in particular those indicated by asterisks on Ex. 1-2: scale degrees C, A, and F, in the first four bars, which receive the dotted half note, the half note, and the whole note. We are probably also sensitive to the melodic shapes, such as the setting of "brown hair," with its beautifully expressive ascending motion that contrasts with the basically descending motion of the preceding music. Even more prominent is the dramatic ascent from F to high F on "borne like a zephyr," which is a lovely example of word painting.[2] In short, although an elementary grasp of scale degree terminology is useful, there is more to understanding and appreciating a melody than can be obtained simply by identifying its scale degree constituents.

Melodic Coordinates

Ex. 1-3 takes an important step toward acquiring a deeper grasp of the special characteristics of "Jeannie." It contains annotations that identify certain key moments in the first two phrases of the song. The first of these moments is simply

Ex. 1-3. "I Dream of Jeannie"

the first note in the melody, called the *headnote*, in this case scale degree 6. The close association of this note and the note that follows it, scale degree 5, which acquires special emphasis because of its long duration, is immediately apparent as well.

In bar 3, because the low C is the lowest note in the entire melody, it is marked "nadir." The *nadir* pitch or note of a song is one of the *melodic coordinates* that are so important to many in American classic popular songs.[3] And in bar 6, setting the first syllable of "zephyr" is another of the melodic coordinates, the highest note of the song, appropriately labelled "apex."

Singled out by the asterisk in bar 2 is B♭, scale degree 4. This special note sets the first syllable of "Jeannie," perhaps the most important key word in the lyrics. Because it is surrounded by two occurrences of A, representing the adjacent scale degrees, we can regard B♭ as a *decoration* of A. In this capacity it is a note of special status in the song, since it is the only such stepwise adjacency, circumscribed by the notes it decorates. In addition, since this portion of "Jeannie" omits scale degree 7 altogether and since scale degree 4, the decorative note,

Ex. 1-4. Pentatonic scale

does not belong to the basic stock of pitches, the foundational scale of the music can be extracted and represented as shown in Ex. 1-4.

Just for the record—and then this exciting information can be stored for later use—the five notes represented as open noteheads in Ex. 1-4 make up the *pentatonic scale*, a basic formation in the classic American popular song repertoire, of which there are many, very many, instances.

Come to me, my mel - an - chol - y ba - by.

Cud - dle up and don't be blue._____

Ex. 1-5. "Melancholy Baby"

Diatonic and Chromatic Melodic Notes

"Diatonic" describes the notes in the natural scale that are specified by the key signature. Thus, the one flat in the key signature for "Jeannie" rests upon the third line of the staff, occupied by letter-name B. Accordingly, every B in the song is to be lowered a half step, and this alteration does not require any additional symbols in the notation. Thus, the melody of "Jeannie" shown in Ex. 1-2 is completely diatonic, consisting of white keys on the keyboard plus B♭.

On the other hand, the melody of "Melancholy Baby," described later in this chapter (Ex. 1-5), contains three signs not in the key signature: two sharp signs and a flat sign. Accordingly, the nondiatonic notes to which these symbols apply are called *chromatic* notes. The first two, F♯ and G♭, are inserted between two diatonic notes, filling in the whole step between F and G. These connectors are called *passing notes*, or, more accurately, *chromatic passing notes*. The C♯ in bar 5 (on "up") stands between two notes of the same kind, D's, and serves as an adjacency to the Ds, just as did B♭ in "Jeannie." Here, however, the adjacency is chromatic. For reasons that fortunately lie deeply buried in the past, sharps and flats other than those in the key signature are called "accidentals." (Of course there is nothing accidental about them; somebody put them there intentionally!)

In a light-hearted vein, Ex. 1-6 uses repetition of diatonic notes to avoid the chromatic notes specified by the accidentals in Ex. 1-5. The reader can judge the aesthetic quality of this emendation compared with the chromatic original. The three repeated notes on "-dle up and" are especially striking in their crudity.

Melodic Contour

Sensitivity to melodic contour is an essential part of listening to classic American popular song: whole steps, half steps, and leaps (or skips) that negotiate intervals larger than the half or whole step contribute to the expressive qualities of a song's melody, sometimes creating melodic contours that are complex. A contour, how-

Come to me, my mel - an - chol - y ba - by.

Cud - dle up and don't be blue. ————

Ex. 1-6. "Melancholy Baby"

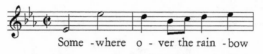

Some -where o - ver the rain -bow

Ex. 1-7. "Over the Rainbow"

ever, may also be short and sweet. For example, the leap at the beginning of Harold Arlen's "Over The Rainbow" that sets "Somewhere," with its upward and outward projection (Ex. 1-7), clearly expresses a celestial destination by its contour. It captured the ears and hearts of millions of Americans in 1939 and in succeeding generations as well.

Melodic Motives

A *melodic motive* is a figure, usually of short duration, which, after its initial statement, is repeated later in the melody, perhaps in its original shape or altered in some recognizable way. Ex. 1-8 displays a two-note motive that occurs in "Jeannie" and consists of the first two notes in the melody, D-C, which initially set "I dream." This motivic item, a fragment of the pentatonic scale (Ex. 1-4), returns, reversed, to set "brown" in bar 3, and reappears again in bars 6–7 where it sets "-yr

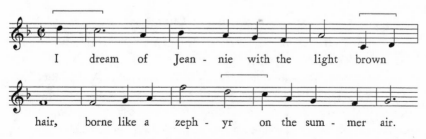

I dream of Jean - nie with the light brown

hair, borne like a zeph - yr on the sum - mer air.

Ex. 1-8. "I Dream of Jeannie"

on." When the motive continues, it unfolds the entire pentatonic scale, ending on the syllable "er" in "summer" at the end of bar 7.[4]

HARMONY

Melody alone does not a song make, at least a classic American popular song. Without harmony, an essential ingredient is lacking. A few basics in this area will enable the reader to follow important parts of the discussions of individual songs in Part II. Let's begin with *chords*. Ex. 1-9 shows the notation for a famous pre–

Ex. 1-9. "Melancholy Baby" harmonized

World War I melody, "My Melancholy Baby," which fairly drips with sentiment but which nevertheless has some very affective *chord changes*. These are notated in two ways on Ex. 1-9: above the upper or treble staff are *chord symbols*, such as A7 in bars 3 and 4, which are fully notated on the lower or bass staff. The chord symbols are standard shorthand for the fully notated chords and are used on the musical examples throughout the present volume for the convenience of the reader.

Major and Minor Chords

We draw a basic distinction between chords that are *major* and those that are *minor*. Note that these designations do not imply a qualitative difference. Minor chords are every bit as good as major chords, sometimes better. Abbreviations are used in connection with the chord symbols to indicate their major or minor affiliations: "min" stands for minor and "maj" for major. Makes sense, doesn't it? For instance, on Ex. 1-9 the chord symbol Dmin is prominently featured in the second four-bar phrase.

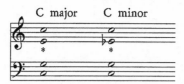

Ex. 1-10. Major and minor chords

There is a very audible difference between the two types of chords. To illustrate, Ex. 1-10 displays a C major chord—so called because C is the lowest note in the bass—which is adjacent to a C minor chord. They differ by only one note: E in the major chord changes to E♭ in the minor chord. However, the difference between the musical effect of a major sonority and that of a minor sonority is remarkable, and in the classic American popular song we find that the expressive purposes to which this contrast is put are just as extraordinary—and, moreover, diversified. For example, although one usually thinks of minor as eliciting a feeling of sorrow, or perhaps at least despondency, there are many counter-instances in the repertoire of American popular song. Irving Berlin's joyous "Blue Skies" (1927) begins on a minor harmony, to cite but one instance.

As usual, lyrics provide clues to expressive interpretation. We can hear the effect of a minor chord in "My Melancholy Baby" (Ex. 1-9) when, in bar 3, the D minor chord sets the line "Cuddle up and don't be blue." Here the minor sonority clearly helps depict "blueness," and generations of Americans have intuitively understood that connection.

Major and Minor Keys

Just as we have major and minor chords we have major and minor keys, familiar to all from works such as Beethoven's Symphony No. 1 in C Major and learned identifications by music critics and classical disc jockeys. For reasons that exceed my powers of explanation, most classic American popular songs are in major keys. Although it begins on a minor sonority, Irving Berlin's "Blue Skies," ends in a major key. The same is true for many other songs. For example, Cole Porter's beautiful love song, "Easy To Love," begins with an A minor chord as though it would continue in the key of A minor, but the actual key turns out to be G major. Songs that sustain a minor key throughout are therefore cause for special attention (and perhaps even alarm).

For our purposes, "key" is synonymous with "tonality" and designates the primary scale and tonic triad to which all the harmonic and melodic events in the song ultimately relate.[5]

Ex. 1-11a. Seventh chords

Seventh Chords

Because they color and enhance the expressive harmony of virtually every song in the repertoire of classic American popular music, seventh chords deserve serious but limited attention. We will deal only with the basic kinds of seventh chord, leaving the more exotic species for later study—in another book.

Dominant Seventh Chord

Seventh chords come in five types: dominant seventh, minor seventh, diminished seventh, half-diminished seventh, and major seventh. Let us consider each type, beginning with the dominant seventh. This chord may be approached, warily, as an arrangement of intervals. Ex. 1-11a shows how we might construct such a chord, beginning with the dominant scale degree G in the key of C (at 1 on Ex. 1-11a). To this note we then add a note a seventh above it, traversing the seven scalar notes beginning on G to arrive on F (G-A-B-C-D-E-F). Notice the neat correspondence of the span of seven scalar notes and the interval of the seventh. Does this seem accidental? I hasten to say that it is not.

Now (at 2 on Ex. 1-11a) we have in place the crucial interval of a seventh (from G to F) that will begin to identify the completed chord as a representative of the dominant seventh *type*. Note that I emphasize "type" here, since dominant sevenths need not begin on the dominant note in the key, but may attach themselves to other scale degrees, as does the A7 in bars 3 and 4 of Ex. 1-9. This A7 is a chord of the dominant seventh *type*, although it is not *the* dominant seventh in the key of C. In fact, the dominant seventh chord in C is the one we are in the process of constructing right now.

To continue, with the interval of the seventh, G-F, firmly in place, as shown in Ex. 1-11a at 2, we need only add two additional notes to complete the arrangement of intervals that will qualify this chord to present itself anywhere in the world as an authentic, bona fide, and certified specimen of the dominant seventh type. Thus, at 3 in Ex. 1-11a we add a note, B, to create the interval of a third above the lowest note, G, sometimes called the "root" of the chord, perhaps reflecting the humble agrarian origins of many Americans. And at 4 in Ex. 1-11a, a final note, D, creates the interval of a fifth above the bass, completing the collection of intervals that forms the dominant seventh chord. Again, remember that this type of chord may occur in contexts where it does not function as *the* dominant seventh chord in the key of a particular song, that is, as a chord constructed upon the scalar dominant note and placed in a context that verifies its dominant function. Unfortunately, harmony, like life, may be interesting but is not always simple.

The chord symbol associated with the harmony at 4 in Ex. 1-11a would be G7. Because only the chord root and the numeric 7 are given, the performer assumes a chord of the dominant seventh type.

Minor Seventh Chord

Many songwriters of the "classic" period of American popular song regarded the minor seventh chord as a conveyor of particularly arresting and beautiful sound, and we shall encounter many instances of this harmony throughout this book.

Construction of the minor seventh chord is straightforward, following a pattern similar to the one described in connection with the dominant seventh chord. Beginning with the seventh that always characterizes the seventh chord species (Ex. 1-11b at 1) we add the note that will create the interval of a third above the

Seventh Third Fifth
(minor)

Ex. 1-11b

root G. However, this third is not a *major* third, as it was in the case of the dominant seventh chord, but a *minor* third, spanning three half steps—specifically, the note B♭. Last, the D at 3 in Ex. 1-11b completes the chord, forming a fifth with the root G, as it did in the dominant seventh chord.

The chord symbol associated with this chord is Gm7, for G minor seventh. As in the case of all the seventh chords, the chord symbol tells only what notes are to be sounded, not how they are arranged vertically.

The next type of seventh chord, the diminished seventh, is a smaller matter—that is, it is a compression of the dominant seventh type. In Ex. 1-11c at 1, we again see the seventh from G to F, mimicking the first stage of construction of the dominant seventh chord (Ex. 1-11a at 1), except that the lower note, G, has been raised by the insertion of the sharp sign, thus shortening the interval

Dim.   Third   Fifth   Dim. triads
seventh

Ex. 1-11c

between that note and the F above it. (I pause momentarily to allow the reader to contemplate this reduction in size.) This interval, which reduces or diminishes the larger seventh of the dominant seventh type, is called, aptly enough, a *diminished seventh*. When the third is added (Ex. 1-11c at 2), then the fifth (Ex. 1-11c at 3), following the pattern of construction used to form the dominant seventh type, we end up with a choice specimen of the diminished seventh chord. Remarkably, it differs by only one note from the dominant seventh chord, but oh, as my mother used to say, what a difference in sound.

On published sheet music, the chord-symbol notation for the diminished seventh varies, but the lead sheets of this book use the symbol "dim7." The symbol for the chord in Ex. 1-11c at 3 would then be G♯dim7, since the lowest note is G♯.

Despite its diminutive size, the diminished seventh chord has been one of the stellar performers in the world of tonal harmony, carrying out heroic tasks in nineteenth-century opera and permeating the improvised piano or organ background music for silent films, in which, with appropriate *tremolando*, it usually accompanied the appearance of the villain. In the context of this book it executes a remarkable variety of colorful roles in the classic American popular song. One reason for the popularity of the diminished seventh chord is its intensification of only two types of interval: the interval that spans three half steps and the interval that spans six half steps. This creates a readily identifiable, powerful, and focused sonority. Further, if we extract the three-note components of this chord—its triads, as it were—we discover that they are all of the same type. Shown at 4 in Ex. 1-11c, these triads are called *diminished triads*.

Half-Diminished Seventh Chord

Now, as the patient reader will shortly see, I have gone to all the trouble of extracting its triads from the hapless diminished seventh chord mainly to explain the name of the fourth and more distinguished member of the seventh-chord aristocracy, the *half-diminished seventh chord*. First, however, let us construct a sample of that type of seventh chord, following the pattern established for the dominant and diminished seventh types—but upside down.

Ex. 1-11d at 1 begins with G, as before. At 2 in Ex. 1-11d, the note a seventh

Ex. 1-11d

below is added (G-F-E-D-C-B-A), framing the new type of chord. Now we proceed just as in the case of the dominant seventh chord, but in the opposite direction. Referring to Ex. 1-11a the reader will see that the next note to be added lies four half-steps *above* G. Therefore, the next note to be added to our nascent half-diminished seventh chord lies four half-steps below: the note Eb (Ex. 1-11d at 3). Similarly, the D *above* G in the dominant seventh chord of Ex. 1-11a at 4 becomes C *below* the G, completing the specimen half-diminished seventh chord.

Despite the appearance of the word "diminished" in the name of this type of seventh chord, its sound differs considerably from that of a diminished seventh chord. In fact, the only sonic connection between the the two chords is the single diminished triad found in the half-diminished seventh chord (Ex. 1-11d at 5). As composer-theorist Milton Babbitt has astutely pointed out, the "half-diminished" seventh chord should be called the "one-third" diminished seventh chord.

The symbol for the half-diminished seventh chord varies. Bear in mind that these symbols are purely practical in intention: they do not show the origin or function of the chord in the music but are merely intended to enable the musician to find the right notes. Thus, the half-diminished seventh chord in Ex. 1-11d at 4 might be labeled Am7−5, which calls for an A minor seventh chord A-C-E-G, but with the fifth lowered, as indicated by the minus sign, so that the correct reading of the chord is A-C-Eb-G, that is, a half-diminished seventh chord built on A.

Whatever its deficiencies might be in the label department, however, the half-diminished seventh chord is in many respects the star of the seventh chord harmonic cast. Many songs in the classic American popular song repertoire reserve it for their most intensely expressive moments, and we shall hear instances of this throughout, including the striking occurrence shown below in Ex. 1-13.

Major Seventh Chord

The fifth and last type of seventh chord, the major seventh, is perhaps the most exotic and, one might even say, mysterious, of the lot. In construction it is identical to the dominant seventh type, except that the interval of the seventh is enlarged by a half step. Comparing Ex. 1-11a at 2 with Ex. 1-11e at 1 we see that

1   2

Seventh   Third
and fifth

Ex. 1-11e

the seventh above the root is now F♯, instead of F. This large interval of a seventh (G to F♯) is called a *major* seventh, compared with the *minor* seventh (G to F) of the dominant seventh type. Completion of the major seventh type, shown in Ex. 1-11e at 2 follows the pattern of the dominant seventh. Our survey of seventh chords is now complete and we can heave a sigh of relief. But afterward I urge you to savor the sonority of the major seventh chord by playing it on a piano, zither, or other suitable instrument.

Real-Life Examples of Seventh Chords

I have borrowed the first two phrases of Gershwin's "Embraceable You" from Chapter 3 to illustrate two of the seventh-chord types discussed above. In bar 2 of Ex. 1-12 we see the chord symbol Gdim7, which specifies a diminished seventh chord above the root G. On the lower staff of bar 2 the chord appears fully notated, as G-B♭-C♯-E, reading from the bottom up. The reader may ask where the diminished seventh is in that chord—a very good question, indeed. Since G, the root, is fixed in place and cannot be altered, the diminished seventh above it should be F♭. A moment's reflection, however, brings the realization that E at the top of the chord has the same sound as F♭—a relation called, I regret to say, *enharmonic equivalence*. In similar fashion, C♯ in the chord stands for its enharmonic equivalent D♭. To invoke a useful cliché, in the final analysis these notational variants do not affect the sound of the harmony at all. Anyone—well, almost anyone—would recognize this chord as an instance of the diminished seventh type.

The chord symbol in bar 3 of Ex. 1-12 specifies D7, a chord of the dominant seventh type. This chord when constructed upward from the root D would appear as D-F♯-A-C. On the lower staff of Ex. 1-12, however, I have arranged the chord so that the lowest note is F♯. I did this to effect a smoother connection from the previous chord, the Gdim7. All the notes of the D7 are present, but in an order different from that in the "textbook example" illustrated in Ex. 1-11a.

Moving along to the second phrase of "Embraceable You," which begins in bar 5 of Ex. 1-12, we find not one, but two chords of the dominant seventh type. The first of these, in bar 6, has the chord symbol F7, specifying a dominant-seventh type chord constructed upward from F. In this instance I have not rearranged the notes of the chord at all, but have simply presented it following the

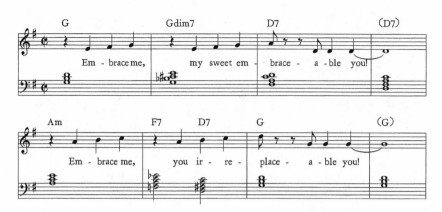

Ex. 1-12. "Embraceable You": Seventh chords

interval pattern that is illustrated in Ex. 1-11a. A D7 chord follows this unusual F7 in bar 6, proceeding to a major triad on G. The startling appearance of F7 here provides an opportunity for a pedagogical point: seventh chords, even unusual ones, may appear unexpectedly in a song.

Yet another type of seventh chord appears in Ex. 1-13 (also drawn from

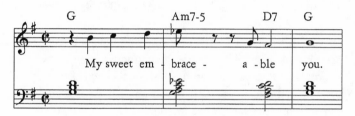

Ex. 1-13. "Embraceable You": Half-diminished seventh chord

Gershwin's "Embraceable You"), the half-diminished seventh in bar 2 of the example. The chord symbol specifies an Am7, which would be A-C-E-G, but with the fifth lowered, as signified by -5. Thus, the chord consists of the notes A-C-Eb-G. Here, and with apologies to the sensitive reader, I have rearranged those notes, again in order to achieve a smoother connection, both to the preceding chord and to the one that follows, which is the D7 we encountered twice in Ex. 1-12.

So far, the real-life examples have illustrated three of the five types of seventh chord: the diminished seventh, the dominant seventh, and the half-diminished seventh. Ex. 1-14, with thanks to Cole Porter, Yale College Class of 1913, pro-

Ex. 1-14. "I've Got You Under My Skin": Seventh chords

vides instances of the remaining two types, beginning with the minor seventh chord in bar 1, symbolized as Fm7 and constructed in pristine arrangement on the lower staff as F-Ab-C-Eb.

The chord symbol for bar 2 of the excerpt shown in Ex. 1-14 specifies Bb7, a dominant-seventh type harmony that would be spelled Bb-D-F-Ab. The alert reader will recognize that the melody contains a note, C, that does not belong to the notes of that chord. My first advice in this case would be to ignore that note, but I will explain its presence. As indicated by the notational tie, this C is held over from the preceding bar, where it belonged to the Fm7 chord. Now in bar 2, when the harmony changes to Bb7, the C, a "non-chord tone," is momentarily in a state of suspension, requiring—indeed, demanding—a motion to a chord tone. This demand is met when the C moves to the Bb7 chord tone Bb on "un-," resolving the moment of expressive tension.

Finally, in bar 3 of Ex. 1-14, the major seventh type puts in an appearance, setting the sensuous word "skin," before the harmony changes to Cm7, a minor seventh chord. Here the major seventh chord, symbolized Ebmaj7, is clearly intended to highlight the keyword "skin," possibly inducing goose bumps to emerge on the epidermis of more susceptible listeners.

It is perhaps not too much of an exaggeration to say that if seventh chords were expunged from the repertoire of classic American popular song, the character of that repertoire would be utterly destroyed. Indeed, the lovely harmonic coloring that seventh chords impart to the music has been intensified and expanded by performers over the years, especially by jazz artists and arrangers, to include ever more elaborate harmonies, some of which are described below.

Added-Note and Altered Chords

Since the topic of altered chords and chords with added notes is vast, I will give only two examples of each type here.[6]

A chord that is perhaps emblematic of the classic American popular song is the chord with added sixth. Ex. 1-15a displays the naive, unadorned C major

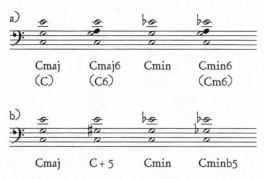

Ex. 1-15. Chords with added notes and altered
chords

chord followed by the same chord with added sixth. Here the added sixth means that the note that lies six notes above the bass in the scale is attached to the chord as a permanent embellishment. In the classic American popular song repertoire this glitzy harmonic item came to be a standard replacement for the simple triad.[7] In the musical examples in this book it is often symbolized simply as C6.

A minor chord (triad) may also take an added sixth, and Ex. 1-15a also displays that harmony, whose chord symbol is Cmin6 or Cm6. The reader should experience this chord's considerably more complex and mysterious effect, compared with the happy-go-lucky major chord with added sixth.[8]

Ex. 1-15b shows two instances of altered chords, both created in the same way, by moving one note of the simple chord to a stepwise adjacency. Thus, moving the note a fifth above the bass of a C major triad up a half step produces a familiar sonority often called the "augmented triad," symbolized C+5, where the plus sign that precedes 5 indicates the raised fifth degree above the bass of the chord. The other altered chord in Ex. 1-15b is more exotic. Here the fifth above the bass of the chord is lowered one half step, producing a new chord, the C+5, where the flat sign that precedes the numeral 5 represents the lowering of the fifth.

Although we cannot generalize concerning the expressive attributes of such altered chords, it is possible to state the obvious: once a chord is altered, its original musical meaning changes radically.

Progression

Harmony in a larger and more important sense consists of more than single unrelated chords, at least in classic American popular songs.[9] The motion of a series of related chords through time and musical space is called *harmonic progression*.

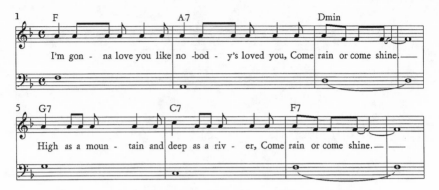

Ex. 1-16. "Come Rain Or Come Shine": Harmonic progression

Again, this is a complicated subject, and one that I will simplify here by briefly discussing just one type of progression. This, however, is a type of progression that is of essential importance to the music we are dealing with, if only because it occurs so often. I refer to progression by the interval of bass fifth, harmonic progression by "fifths-chain."[10] Ex. 1-16 (from Harold Arlen's "Come Rain Or Come Shine") clarifies.[11] In terms of harmony alone, the music of the first four-bar phrase moves from an F major chord through an A7 chord to the goal D minor harmony at the end of the phrase. The second four-bar phrase begins in bar 5 on a G7 chord, passes through a C7 chord, and ends on the F7 chord at the end of this phrase. What makes this a coherent and logical progression are the intervals that join the bass notes. After the initial tonic F, each bass note moves to the next by descending fifth: from A to D is a fifth, from D to G is a fifth, and so on, until the bass reaches the final F. The tonic F major chord occurs at the beginning and end of the progression, and may be said to enclose it. Ex. 1-17 summarizes.

Ex. 1-17. "Come Rain Or Come Shine": Bass
motion by fifth

Notice that the chords above each bass note in Ex. 1-16 have the same name as the bass note, except that the quality of the chord is not determined by the bass. In the passage shown in Ex. 1-16, it so happens that each chord is a seventh chord, with the numeral 7 in the chord symbol, with the D minor chord being an exception.

With this brief introduction we leave the very large subject of harmony, to return to it in many small ways during the discussions of individual songs.

FORM

"Form" in music is one of those topics over which much ink has been spilled for a very long time.[12] For our purposes a brief introduction will suffice.[13] *Form* consists of the succession of musical units that break up the flow of the music and, at the same time, cohere to unify the entire song. We will begin with small musical units and proceed to larger ones. First, here is an example to work with (Ex. 1-18).

The music displayed in Ex. 1-18 is the complete opening section, or *Verse*, of a song by Harry Warren that is discussed later in this book. Each line of the lyrics corresponds neatly to what in the terminology of form is called a *phrase*,

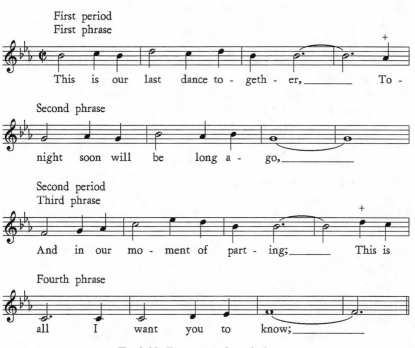

Ex. 1-18. Form: periods and phrases

consisting in this case of four bars of music. Indeed, the phrase that comprises exactly four bars is a basic unit in the classic American popular song, and in Ex. 1-18, we have four clear and carefully labeled instances of it. Notice that each phrase ends with a long duration (involving more than one bar), clearly delimiting its span. Harmony, omitted from Ex. 1-18, also assists in defining the extent of the phrase. In an uncertain world it is gratifying to know that we can almost always count on the four-bar phrase as the norm in the classic American popular song repertoire.

In determining the end of a phrase, novices sometimes become confused. In Ex. 1-18, for instance, there are additional shorter notes following the long-held notes at the ends of the first and second phrases. These notes, indicated by "+", belong to the upcoming phrase, not to the phrase that has just finished, and are variously called "upbeats" or "pickups." But whereas the notation might be momentarily confusing, the musical division is virtually always crystal clear because of rhythm, harmony, and, of course, the lyrics. The phrase proper always begins with the first bar of a four-bar phrase.

We are not through yet. The four phrases of Ex. 1-18 coalesce to form a still larger unit, the *period*. This term is part of the conventional nomenclature of form, sanctified by time and usage (do not blame the author, please). Again, and perhaps obviously so, the period in classic American popular songs normally consists of two four-bar phrases.

In the parsing of form shown in Ex. 1-18 we see that there are two periods, appropriately labeled First period and Second period. The larger unit, comprising the entire Verse of this song, is called a *double period*. Makes sense, doesn't it?

One more refinement and we will have exhausted this topic. Notice that the two four-bar phrases of the first period in Ex. 1-18 are almost the same rhythmically and melodically, except that the second phrase unfolds at a lower pitch level. Phrases that are very similar in this way form periods that are called *parallel periods* because their constituent phrases are "parallel," that is, almost identical. By comparison, the phrases of the second period in this example resemble each other somewhat with respect to rhythm, but their melodic contours differ radically. Phrases of this kind form periods that are called *contrasting periods*. Once again, we encounter a verbal synthesis that represents a triumph of the human imagination. Phrases form periods. Phrases that are contrasting form contrasting periods, while parallel phrases form parallel periods.

Although it may seem a bit cumbersome at first, the traditional terminology of musical form will be very convenient in discussing various features of the songs covered in this book. The language of "phrases" and "periods" also helps to remind us that each song consists of a succession of integral units that contribute to its total effect and expressivity. For the listener who is cognizant of formal components, the flow of the song becomes sharper, more coherent; hence its aesthetic and emotional impact is more intense. Like sport metaphors ("end run" comes to mind), the jargon of musical form not only comes in handy, but it also gives the user that certain aura of being "in the know."

The Verse

As I indicated earlier, the music in Ex. 1-18 is the Verse of Harry Warren's "There Will Never Be Another You." I don't know the origin of the term "verse," but the introductory function of the formal section it designates derives from the the operatic recitative that traditionally precedes an aria. Indeed, the modern verse shares some characteristics with that ancient form. First and foremost, it is intended as an introduction to the Refrain, or main part of the song, and therefore sets the mood in terms of tempo, dynamics, and style.[14] More often than not its melody consists of intentionally stereotyped and repeated rhythmic figures, as in Ex. 1-18, is of limited vocal range, and does not feature the melodic coordinates previously discussed. Moreover, the length of the modern verse is almost always sixteen bars, following a tradition established in nineteenth-century popular songs.[15]

The artistic quality of the verse varies. Some songwriters often did not include verses—for example, Irving Berlin and Jerome Kern. The verseless song is particularly characteristic of songs composed for motion pictures, and we have several examples in this book. Some verses are routine and seem to have been tacked on as an afterthought. Others begin to approach the Refrain in terms of musical interest and attractiveness. That is particularly true of George Gershwin's verses, which are sometimes refrain-like. "How Long Has This Been Going On" comes to mind, but there are many others. Like most of the songwriters of his era, Gershwin composed the Verse only after the Refrain was completed. (The implications of this process are discussed later.) In the best instances, the Verse may also contain surprising and abrupt changes of key, a practice perhaps going back to early Broadway days, where it was developed with the intention of capturing the attention of a possibly drowsy audience.

Parts of the Song

The complete song in the classic American popular song repertoire consists of Verse and Refrain, possibly preceded by an instrumental introduction and ending with a short section or coda:

Introduction		4 bars
Verse		16 bars
Refrain, consisting of		
Chorus 1	(A)	16 bars
Bridge	(B)	8 bars
Chorus 2	(A)	8 bars
Coda	(extension)	2 bars

Of the two main parts of the song, Verse and Refrain, the Refrain is the more complicated. It consists of a double period designated Chorus 1 that precedes the Bridge, the Bridge itself, and a single period called Chorus 2. In some cases the song may end with a coda or extension.

The above table models the ideal form, and of course there are modifications and exceptions. In general, however, the classic American popular song describes the pattern ABA, or statement-departure-return. If the middle section is sufficiently independent, for example, if it is based on a new key or features a radically new melody, it is called the *Bridge*. The formal patterns vary. Three common patterns are:

1)	2)	3)
A 8 bars	A 8 bars	A 8 bars
A 8 bars	B 8 bars	B 8 bars
B 8 bars	A 8 bars	A 8 bars
A 8 bars	A 8 bars	C 8 bars

Although the first of these patterns, AABA, is probably the most common, since it bears the nickname "popular song form," the third pattern, ABAC, is perhaps the most interesting, since it involves new music at the end of the song, albeit music that is usually related motivically to earlier parts of the song. Gershwin's "Embraceable You" may be cited as an instance of the ABAC form.

All three patterns, however, have something in common, a trait that is well known even to music critics: they are all thirty-two bars in length, and each part is eight bars long. Thus, the four-bar phrase and the eight-bar period are the primary building blocks of the classic American popular song repertoire. In the face of such a high degree of uniformity it is absolutely amazing that songs of such remarkable variety were produced between 1925 and 1950.

A Sample Refrain

Although we will have occasion to sample all three patterns, and others, let us take a moment to examine a complete Refrain, that of the Harry Warren song, "There Will Never Be Another You," that was used to illustrate the Verse.

Ex. 1-19. "There Will Never Be Another You": Form of refrain

Ex. 1-19 is laid out in four-bar phrases to make the succession of parts more visible. In the descriptive language introduced above, Part A consists of an eight-bar parallel period that sets the first two lines of the lyrics:

1 There will be many other nights like this
2 And I'll be standing here with someone new

Part B begins at bar 9, preceded by the pickup "There" at the end of bar 8:

3 There will be other songs to sing,
4 Another fall, another spring,
5 But there will never be another you.

Part B extends through bar 16, and we will call it a contrasting period, although the beginning of the second four-bar phrase at bar 13 resembles that of the first, at bar 9. Both phrases begin with a descending contour, in direct contrast to the beginnings of the two phrases of Part A. Notice that Part B includes three lines of the lyrics, a kind of compression, expressing a feeling of urgency.

Here is an interesting question. Should Part B be called the Bridge? Although, in the absence of harmony, we cannot make a firm decision, it seems that this part lacks rhythmic individuality. For example, bars 9 and 10 are rhythmically identical to bars 1 and 2. On the basis of that evidence alone, I would not elevate Part B to the status of a Bridge.[16]

Part A now returns at bar 17, and the repetition is exact with respect to the melody. Only the lyrics change. It is a textbook example of a repeated A section, sometimes, incidentally, written A', where the prime indicates modification of some kind, even though section A' otherwise bears a strong resemblance to its predecessor, A.

The first phrase of Part C begins with three bars that are identical to the first three bars of Part B. Thereafter, the melody is new. In the ABAC pattern, of which this refrain is an instance, the incorporation of elements from the B section into the C section is common. However, since C is not simply a repetition of B in its entirety, it qualifies as a distinct section and receives its own letter designation.

In the broadest view, form describes the shape of music as it is influenced by melody, harmony, and rhythm. And in the case of song, the lyrics play an important role as well since, as we shall see, they interact with the other musical features and may deeply affect our response to the music. In the unfolding of these musical shapes certain strategic moments play a fundamental role in giving the song its character and in conveying its message: the beginnings, the endings, and the climaxes. I give special attention to those moments in the individual song discussions, which also include the conventional parts and a listing of the complete lyrics at the beginning of each.

LYRICS

When listening to a classic American popular song we necessarily engage the mysterious expressive code of harmony and melody upon which the songwriter has drawn, and the marriage of note and word often so beautifully expressed through the artistry of the lyricist.[17]

However, this idealized synergistic relation of text and music sometimes elicits skepticism or at least puzzlement. In its simplest form we often hear the ancient question: Which came first, the words or the music? In the case of the classic American popular song the answer is unequivocal: the music. This remarkable situation is exactly the reverse of the chronology of the European art song, where music invariably sets texts, sometimes poetic texts that may have existed for centuries.[18] Popular song lyrics, on the other hand, are customized products, produced on demand to fit music that has usually been written to perform a particular role in a theatrical production (musical theater or motion picture) or to conform to a particular genre, such as the amatory or comic, intended for the sheet music market.[19]

So remarkable is this music-first rule that in discussing lyrics and music in connection with specific songs later on, I sometimes ignore the chronological priority of the music in the creative process, imagining for purposes of explanation that text and music emerged simultaneously. Looking at this provocative issue in another way, it seems impossible that the music of, say, George Gershwin's "Embraceable You" ever existed without Ira Gershwin's words. But it did, and it does, in instrumental performances, especially by jazz musicians, many of whom may know few of the words beyond the title of the song.

Nevertheless, when we approach popular song lyrics it is important to recognize that, unlike poetry, they came into existence as music-dependent productions. This suggests that the sonic qualities of lyrics are often of importance and interest—perhaps to an even greater extent than they are in high-art poetry. Similarly, rhythmic features have to be interpreted with reference to the rhythms of the musical configurations to which they correspond.

For all these reasons, lyrics are not the same as poetry, although they may share many characteristics with their more artistic sisters. This does not mean, however, that we cannot consider lyrics as self-standing objects and study their special attributes. Indeed, to do so is very often enlightening, adding a new dimension to the music. For that very basic reason I will give special attention to the lyrics of each song.

Words set to music, the arrangement that prevails in the classic American popular song repertoire, have two aspects: the *semantic* and the *sonic*, two sides of the same coin. Under the rubric sonic I include the internal connections created by vowels (*rhyme* being the most obvious) and consonants (*alliteration*), as well as more elusive connections such as *near-rhymes*—for example, the end rhyming words "bliss is" and "missus" at the end of the Verse in Arthur Schwartz's "I Guess I'll Have To Change My Plan." In the area of semantic relations, one should ask how the text relates to such musical events as the moment of occurrence of one of the melodic coordinates discussed previously, or, more generally, how individual words contribute to the basic idea of the text. Speaking of which, we shall encounter instances of *word painting*, a traditional feature of songs that goes far back in music history, whereby the contours and rhythms of the melody, or special harmonic effects, assist in the depiction of an idea that is presented by the lyrics.

Popular song lyrics in this repertoire often utilize two variants on the traditional *end rhyme*, the placement of rhyming words at the ends of lines. These are *inner rhymes*, where rhyming words occur within the line, perhaps in addition to end rhymes, and *internal rhymes,* which involve rhyming syllables within words. A particularly charming instance of the latter occurs in Lorenz Hart's lyrics for Richard Rodgers's "Manhattan": "Summer journeys to Niag'ra / And to other places aggra-vate all our cares." Here the two-syllable succession "-ag'ra" in "Niag'ra" is repeated as "aggra-" in "aggravate," strongly reinforcing the humorous idea that a trip to Niagara Falls might be a less than felicitous event.

Song Titles and Genres

Song titles are naturally part of the lyrics. Indeed, they occupy key positions in the lyrics most of the time, either at the beginning, as in Vernon Duke's "Autumn In New York," or strategically placed for maximum impact at the end of an initial phrase, as in Irving Berlin's "Let Yourself Go."

Categories or genres in classic American popular songs resemble those in art songs, but of course the lyrics of the popular song are more straightforward, lacking complex metaphorical structures and, for the most part, allusions. Perhaps the fullest category is the love song or ballad in which the lyrics range from rueful to passionate. In the passionate category, Cole Porter's "I've Got You Under My Skin," included in this volume, is a prime example. Ironic treatments of love are not difficult to find; Porter's "What Is This Thing Called Love" exemplifies this type of song. And of course there are happy songs, such as Harold Arlen's joyous "I've Got The World On A String." On quite another wavelength are the few depressing songs, such as the Ellington-Strayhorn piece, "Something To Live For."

Although high on the list of human emotions, jealousy is not, strangely enough, among the frequent *topoi.* Still, it may be a subtheme in a number of songs. Irving Berlin's "Change Partners" represents that category. Finally, the torch song represents a very large category, with many subcategories. Although none of the songs on the CD qualifies as a true torch song, several contain lyrics that make the description "torchy" apt. Examples of true torch songs, both by Harold Arlen, are "One For My Baby (And One More For The Road), from 1943, with Johnny Mercer lyrics, and "The Man That Got Away," from 1954, with Ira Gershwin lyrics.

There has been a marked decline in the number of eye-catching song titles with a humorous bent, such as the folksy "My Home Town Is A One-Horse Town —But It's Big Enough For Me" (1920), the slightly naughty "Who Ate Napoleons With Josephine When Bonaparte Was Away?" (1920), or the ingenious "I Gave You Up Just Before You Threw Me Down" (1922). One can only imagine what the music of these songs must have been like, since they did not survive their titles.

Ex. 1-20. "Michael, Row The Boat Ashore": Rhythm

RHYTHM

This brief section will introduce terminology that will be used in the discussions of specific songs.

Ex. 1-20 ("Michael, Row The Boat Ashore") illustrates some basic ideas. At the beginning of the music the 4/4 time or *meter signature* describes the fixed grid of pulses, or meter, that will underlie the variable rhythms of the music. The lower numeral in this signature tells us that the metrical unit is notated as a quarter note or its equivalent (if the lower numeral were an 8, then the metrical unit would be an eighth note, and so on), while the upper numeral gives the number (4) of such notes, or beats, in each bar. The typical waltz, for example has the meter signature 3/4, signifying that each complete measure consists of three quarter notes or their equivalent duration—such as a dotted half note.

Meter is fixed, rhythm is variable.[20] The way in which the durations of the notes that fill a measure are deployed varies depending on the song. In "Michael, Row The Boat Ashore" the metrical pulses, four per bar, are aligned above the staff of Ex. 1-20. Bars 1–2 and 5–6 are identical with respect to rhythm (*not* counting the "upbeat" incomplete measure at the beginning of bar 1). In the rhythmic pattern of bar 1, "row" and "a-" have the same duration. The dotted quarter of "row" is the same as three eighth notes, and the same holds for the eighth tied to quarter of "a-." Above bar 1, the numbers show where the regular succession of metrical beats fall: on "row," between "row" and "the," on "boat," and after the syllable "a-" of "ashore." On the separate staff below bar 1 I have shown the rhythmic pattern as it would be if it were regularized to conform to the meter. Here the syllable "a-" of "ashore" falls squarely on metrical beat 4, whereas in the actual song, "a-" comes in "too soon," anticipating the metrical pulse and pushing the rhythm forward. This occurrence, so typical of American popular song and exemplifying an African-American origin, is known as *syncopation*. "Michael, Row The Boat Ashore" provides a particularly effective illustration since it combines bars which contain syncopation (bars 1, 5, and 7) with bars in which the melodic notes fall precisely on metrical beats (bars 2, 3, 4, 6, and 8). The syncopation in penultimate bar 7 is particularly striking, since the rhythm supports a single syllable, "lu-," and only the first note falls on a metrical beat.

The Charleston Pattern

As I suggested above, syncopated patterns are characteristic of the American popular song idiom. Some have even acquired names. The "Charleston" is an example.

Ex. 1-21 gives the notation for the Charleston rhythmic pattern, a rhythm that originated in Charleston, South Carolina, and swept the country in 1924 as a dance craze of the same name. As is evident when the pattern is clapped or

Charles-ton   Charles-ton

Ex. 1-21. Charleston rhythmic pattern

otherwise realized, the tied eighth note anticipates the metrical second beat in the "cut time" or *alla breve* bar, which contains two half-note beats. This gives a considerable impetus to the second metrical pulse and propels the music and the dancers forward to new heights of ecstasy. Ex. 1-21 shows that the rhythmic pattern fits the two syllables of "Charleston" exactly, emphasizing the first syllable of the word and perhaps suggesting a southern linguistic inflection as well.

In fact, the most important characteristic of rhythm in the songs with which this volume is concerned is this: the melodic rhythms follow the natural accentual patterns and groupings of English (American) speech. This generalization may seem somewhat circular, since it is the lyricist's assignment of words to melodic components that makes the rhythmic patterns seem natural. Still, the musical rhythms alone invite a natural speech setting, and of course natural speech in a popular idiom is expected and even demanded for artistic as well as commercial reasons.

Dance Rhythms

In connection with the individual songs, I will point out the occurrence of dance rhythms, especially rhythms associated with what, by the thirties, had become

the national ballroom dance, the fox-trot. Also rhythms associated with professional dancing, which became familiar through dance numbers in musicals and
(later) in movies, were taken up in songs. I refer in particular to the dotted, long-
short-long rhythms of the tap dance, as well as the triplet rhythm so characteristic
of that genre.

Harmony-Rhythm Analogs

In a more abstract context, the bending of meter through syncopated rhythm and
prolonged subdivisions of the metrical beat finds an analogy in the bending of
traditional harmonic sonorities through chromatic alteration and the accretion
of foreign notes to familiar harmonies—a process that I touched upon earlier.

CHAPTER TWO

Songs from the Twenties

■

GEORGE GERSHWIN, "FASCINATING RHYTHM"
Lyrics by Ira Gershwin
CD Track 1

Ex. 2-1. "Fascinating Rhythm": Leadsheet

LYRICS
Verse

Got a little rhythm,
A rhythm, a rhythm
That pit-a-pats through my brain.

So darn persistent,
The day isn't distant
When it'll drive me insane.
Comes in the morning
Without any warning,
And hangs around all day.
I'll have to sneak up to it,
Someday, and speak up to it,
I hope it listens when I say:

Refrain
Chorus I
A (eight-bar period)

"Fascinating Rhythm
You've got me on the go!
Fascinating Rhythm
I'm all aquiver.
What a mess you're making!
The neighbors want to know
Why I'm always shaking
Just like a flivver.

Bridge
B (eight-bar period)

Each morning I get up with the sun,
(Start a hopping, never stopping)
To find at night, no work has been done.
I know that

Chorus 2
A (eight-bar period)

Once it didn't matter
But now you're doing wrong:
When you start to patter,
I'm so unhappy.
Won't you take a day off?
Decide to run along

Somewhere far away off,
And make it snappy!

C (eight-bar period)

Oh, how I long to be
The man I used to be!
Fascinating Rhythm,
Oh, won't you stop picking on me!"

This famous song comes from *Lady, Be Good!*, the equally famous show of 1924, starring Fred Astaire and his sister, Adele, which opened on Broadway right in the middle of the post–World War I period. Among the events on the international scene in 1924: Stalin's ascendance to power; Britain recognized the U.S.S.R.; France left the German industrial Ruhr Valley; and Hitler was sentenced to five years in prison for the Munich *Putsch.* In the United States, the new immigration law excluded Japanese, while, in a gesture of gracious condescension, Congress declared native-born Indians citizens. The country was shocked by the Teapot Dome scandal, and the G.O.P. nominated Calvin Coolidge, who during his campaign asserted: "This is a business country, and it wants a business government."

Despite an emphasis upon the pragmatics of business and government, the arts in America were doing well. O'Neill's *Desire under the Elms* opened on Broadway, as did Maxwell Anderson's *What Price Glory?* Serge Koussevitsky was appointed conductor of the Boston Symphony, and Georgia O'Keeffe achieved recognition as a painter of great originality.

Music was in a state of flux, with avant-gardists Carl Ruggles and Henry Cowell attracting some attention while George Gershwin attracted considerable attention, both positive and negative, through the premiere of his *Rhapsody in Blue*, a jazz-influenced orchestral work.[1] Indeed, this period is often characterized as the "Jazz Age," for it was then that the rhythmic vitality of jazz, together with its characteristic harmonies, began to invade the music of the Broadway stage, influencing dance styles and even couture. "Fascinating Rhythm" epitomizes this extraordinary development in American popular song, which was to bring about changes that exerted a considerable influence in the years to come.[2]

Why "Fascinating Rhythm" Is Fascinating

From a rhythmic standpoint "Fascinating Rhythm" is a remarkable musical artifact even today. It is by no means a simple pastiche of existing jazz elements, but

Ex. 2-2. "Fascinating Rhythm": Six-note pattern normalized

rather a distillation of a primary rhythmic characteristic of jazz embedded in a totally new framework.[3]

What makes the rhythm forever fascinating is the way in which it deflects our expectations of regularity, a remarkable celebration of the phenomenon of syncopation illustrated earlier in "Michael, Row The Boat Ashore" (Ex. 1-20).[4]

Ex. 2-2 shows the six-note melodic pattern of "Fascinating Rhythm" as it would appear in a regular four-bar phrase. I suggest that the reader play, sing, or hear the musical examples mentally. As I have indicated by the numbers above the notes in Ex. 2-2, each bar in "cut time" (*alla breve*) contains eight eighth-note pulses, the first six of which are sounding notes, while the last two are silences (rests).

The first three bars of Ex. 2-2 conform exactly to the two pulses of the notated meter and are therefore identical. To bring the pattern to an end, so that it conforms to the four-bar norm, in the final bar the last two notes of the six-note pattern and the two rests coalesce in the half-note Bb. In this way, the eight-pulse rhythmic pattern, which consists of six eighth notes and two rests, and the two-pulse regular meter correspond exactly. As a result, the large half-note metrical pulses, represented by numerals 1 and 2 at the top of each bar in Ex. 2-2, always correspond to the notes F and Bb, as Ex. 2-3 illustrates.

Ex. 2-3. "Fascinating Rhythm": Metrical pulses of normalized
version

Contrasting radically with the music in Ex. 2-2, Ex. 2-4 shows Gershwin's actual deployment of the six-note pattern. Now, instead of the *two* rests that fill out the eight-pulse bar, a *single* rest follows each six-note pattern. As a result, the

Ex. 2-4. "Fascinating Rhythm": Real six-note pattern

Ex. 2-5. "Fascinating Rhythm": Metrical pulses of real pattern

notes that fall on the metrical beats form a different pattern in each bar (Ex. 2-5). In the first bar they are F-B♭, in the second A♭-B♭, and so on. By shortening by one eighth note the silence that separates each pitch pattern rest, the headnote of each pattern hops over the bar line sooner than expected, deflecting the regular pattern to produce a large-scale precipitate pattern of syncopation that spans the entire four-bar phrase and generates a wonderful feeling of energy. It is the effect of this obsessive and "fascinating rhythm" that the lyrics describe. Just imagine, a whole song devoted to a rhythm!

But how do we know that the meter is actually present as the regular two-beat pattern with which the seven-beat syncopation interacts? In other words, how is the meter represented in the music? The answer lies in the chords that Gershwin wrote to accompany the melody. Ex. 2-6 shows that these chords form a regular pattern that conforms exactly to the meter and against which the errant melody pursues its wayward path.[5]

Thus, it is the constant tension over three bars, followed by the denouement in the last bar, that creates the interest and "fascination" of the pattern, a fascination that has lasted over many years and that is evident in the performance of our artists on the accompanying compact disc.

The position of Gershwin's "Fascinating Rhythm" as the first song to be discussed is not merely the result of happenstance; the songs in the book are arranged by period, beginning with songs of the 1920s, and "Fascinating Rhythm" is the earliest of those selected to represent that period. At the same time, however, "Fascinating Rhythm" serves nicely as a reminder of the basic role of rhythm

Ex. 2-6. "Fascinating Rhythm": Chordal accompaniment

and of the various forms of syncopation, in particular, in the repertoire of popular song with which this book is concerned.

The Refrain Lyrics

Perhaps the most striking feature of Ira Gershwin's lyrics for the refrain is its virtual detachment from the syncopated rhythmic pattern of the notes: with one exception the natural accentual patterns of the language are preserved against the agitated and disruptive note pattern. Here is the first stanza of the lyrics, with italics indicating the placement of accents.

> *a* "*Fas*cinating *Rhy*thm
> *b* You've *got* me on the *go!*
> *a* Fasci*nat*ing Rhythm
> *c* I'm all a*qui*ver.

As the italicized syllables indicate, only in the third line does the underlying two-pulse meter shift the accent of the lyric "Fascinating" from the first to the third syllable. Ex. 2-7 shows the full music notation of the first eight bars of the song's melody.

As always, Ira Gershwin's rhyme schemes are ingenious. In this instance the rhyme scheme unifies the two four-line stanzas by using the pattern *abac* in both. Therefore, the lyrics of the second stanza, shown below, are a varied repetition of the first.

> *a* What a mess you're making!
> *b* The neighbors want to know

Ex. 2-7. "Fascinating Rhythm": Bars 1–8

a Why I'm always shaking
c Just like a flivver.

Line 4 in the second stanza attracts special attention because of the word "flivver," which rhymes "aquiver." This term, an American coinage, refers to a motorized vehicle of uncertain provenance and qualifications, which, when coaxed into action probably by means of a hand crank, shudders reluctantly during the warm-up period.

The music of the first eight bars (Ex. 2-7) links seamlessly with the music of the following eight bars, which make up the Bridge (Ex. 2-8).

The lyrics of this eight-bar Bridge period clearly illustrate the "patter" to which the lyrics refer in the return to the A section of the Refrain (bar 17). It merely forms a part of the singer's whimsical indictment. Now, however, the rhyme scheme is the simpler *abba*, with the two inner lines referring obliquely yet graphically to the action implied by the "flivver" metaphor:

a Each morning I get up with the sun,
b Start a hopping
b Never stopping
a To find at night, no work has been done.

All good things must come to an end, as they say, and repetition in music usually bends to the requirement for closure, which, in the case of the American

Ex. 2-8. "Fascinating Rhythm": Bridge

Ex. 2-9. "Fascinating Rhythm": Close

popular song idiom, means completion of the thirty-two-bar paradigm. Ex. 2-9 shows how Gershwin constructs the close of the song. The first four bars of final section C, beginning in bar 25, refer back to the music of section B (bars 9–16), while the second and last four bars refer to the theme from the opening music. The lyrics of this final section consist of an appropriately humorous final effort to enlist the listener's sympathy for the deleterious effects the "fascinating rhythm" is having upon the singer.

    a Oh, how I long to be the man I used to be!
    b Fascinating Rhythm,
    a Oh, won't you stop picking on me?" [6]

In the musical setting of these lines, the melody ascends step by step from "how" to reach its apex on the high F of "used" in bar 27. The histrionic implication of this gesture is very characteristic of the musical theater, not only of Gershwin's era but of later periods as well. The song then ends with a final statement and variation on the 6-note theme of "Fascinating Rhythm," arriving firmly on the tonic note E♭, presumably releasing the singer from the obsessive pattern that has threatened to ruin his life!

Verse

Up to now I have neglected the Verse of "Fascinating Rhythm," (Ex. 2-10) but not because it is negligible. It has its own charm and interest, beginning with the long–short dotted figure (dotted eighth note followed by sixteenth note) that per-

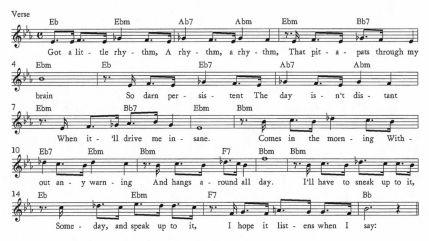

Ex. 2-10. *"Fascinating Rhythm": Verse*

sists throughout. This toe-tapping and jazzy item would have been understood as very "rhythmic" in Gershwin's day and even now. It is not, however, the fascinating rhythm that is the subject of the Refrain of this song, but a rhythm of a more ordinary variety, one unlikely to induce the terrifying agitation the lyrics describe in the Refrain.

Although the double period sixteen-bar form of the Verse is straightforward and conventional, its melodic content is unusual. Disregarding the difference in rhythm, the melodic figures of the Verse are strongly imitative of the melody of the Refrain: the notes that set "Got a little rhy -" (Eb-F-Gb) span the same interval, a minor third, as the opening two notes of the Refrain.

In the Verse, however, the Gb that sets "rhy -" of the key word "rhythm" has another meaning. It is the minor or blue third in the key of the song, Eb major. As might be expected, another blue note, the lowered seventh scale degree, Db, turns up at the beginning of the second period in the Verse (bar 9), where it first sets "morn -." In the Refrain, this same note returns at the beginning of bar 5 (Ex. 2-1), initiating the lyrics "What a mess you're making." The listener should have no difficulty relating the three notes in that melodic fragment (Bb-Db-C) to the three notes in bar 9 of the Verse that set the lyrics "Comes in the morning." Indeed, this melodic figure replicates the figure in bar 1 of the verse at a higher pitch level—known to musicians as a *transposition*.

There are other similarities between the melodies of Verse and Refrain in this song. For instance, the first long note, the Bb that sets "brain" in bar 4 of the Verse, sets the key word "rhythm" in the Refrain. More striking, the apex of the Verse, the F that sets "day" in bar 12, is the apex of the Refrain, setting "used" in bar 27.

The Verse of "Fascinating Rhythm" presents, in essence, some of the prominent features of the Refrain. And, as we shall see in the other two Gershwin songs discussed below, this melodic linkage of Verse and Refrain is very characteristic of that songwriter's music, as it is of many of the songs in this repertoire.

■

RICHARD RODGERS, "MANHATTAN"
Lyrics by Lorenz Hart
CD Track 2

LYRICS
Verse

Summer journeys to Niag'ra,
And to other places
Aggravate all our cares;
We'll save our fares;
I've a cozy little flat
In what is known as old Manhattan,
We'll settle down
Right here in town.

Ex. 2-11. "Manhattan": Leadsheet

Refrain

Chorus I

We'll have Manhattan,
The Bronx and Staten Island too;
It's lovely going through the Zoo;

B

It's very fancy
On old Delancey Street, you know;
The subway charms us so,
When balmy breezes blow
To and fro;

Chorus 2

And tell me what street
compares with Mott Street in July,
Sweet push carts gently gliding by;

C

The great big city's a wond'rous toy
Just made for a girl and boy,
We'll turn Manhattan into an isle of joy.

In 1925, Florida passed a law requiring daily reading of the Bible in public schools. Forty-five thousand members of the Ku Klux Klan marched in Washington, D.C. In July, Tennessee public school teacher John Scopes was placed on trial and convicted for teaching Darwin's theory of evolution. President Coolidge reduced the White House budget by replacing paper cups with glasses, reducing the number of towels in lavatories, and rationing food in the kitchen.

In the movies (silent of course), Charlie Chaplin starred in the hilarious comedy *The Gold Rush*. A key scene shows him as the starving central character meticulously preparing and then eating the sole of his shoe. The original *Ben-Hur* starred Ramon Novarro. The original *Phantom of the Opera* starred Lon Chaney. Top stars at the box office included Rudolph Valentino, Douglas Fairbanks, Mary Pickford, Charlie Chaplin, Harold Lloyd, Gloria Swanson, and Lillian Gish.

Radio became the communications medium of choice for a huge number of Americans. According to a Library of Congress estimate, the radio audience was 50 million strong, a large portion of the population at that time. The all-electric phonograph (as distinct from the windup or battery-run type) began to attract massive public attention, and the recording industry took off. Louis Armstrong and Duke Ellington made their first recordings, while Lawrence Welk formed a new band that played "society music."

In the field of modern concert music of avant-garde persuasion, Edgar Varèse composed *Intégrales*, Henry Cowell *The Banshee*. Igor Stravinsky performed his *Concerto for Piano and Winds* (which premiered in France in 1924) with the Boston Symphony Orchestra. To an audience with eclectic tastes, George Gershwin presented his *Concerto in F for Piano and Orchestra* in New York.

The Metropolitan Museum of Art recorded the largest attendance in its history: over one million visitors. John D. Rockefeller endowed the institution that became the present-day medieval Cloisters in New York City. Landmarks in American literature: F. Scott Fitzgerald's *The Great Gatsby* and Theodore Dreiser's *An American Tragedy*. Sinclair Lewis won the Pulitzer Prize for literature with *Arrowsmith*. In professional athletics, Bill Tilden won his fifth straight tennis singles championship, and burlesque star Carrie Finnel attracted considerable attention from an enthusiastic audience by twirling tassels from her breasts and buttocks.

American patterns of courtship were changing, with the automobile beginning to replace the parlor as the venue of choice for romantic undertakings. Ever susceptible to fads, the public indulged in limerick contests, the collecting of baseball cards, the worship of athletic heroes, and marathons of various kinds, among them dancing, talking, and flagpole sitting. And of course musical theater flourished in its natural habitat, the borough of Manhattan of New York City, where Richard Rodgers and Lorenz Hart took a big step toward the stellar position they ultimately came to occupy.

The Birth and Early History of "Manhattan"

Rodgers and Hart wrote "Manhattan" in 1922 for a show called *Winkle Town*, which was never produced.[7] Nevertheless, as it turned out, the song became a landmark in their fledgling career, setting the stage for their long and remarkable presence on the American musical scene. Three years later, when the song was included in the review "Garrick Gaieties," its popularity was instantaneous. Rodgers has related his impression at the end of the first performance: "I turned around to look at the audience; everyone was standing. Not standing to leave, just standing. Not just standing, either. Standing and clapping, cheering, yelling, stomping, waving and whistling. I turned back to the orchestra and had the boys strike up 'Manhattan.' The cast sang it. The musicians sang it. Even the audience sang it."[8]

Why this spontaneous reaction? I will try to answer that question in one way by considering an important aspect of the melody, its constituent figures, or motives, and by pointing out some of the ways in which Hart's ingenious lyrics enhance them. At the same time this provides an opportunity to deal with some general aspects of the melodic details that are so important to any song and to the listener who wishes to delve below the surface.

Melodic Motives

Ex. 2-12 shows the first eight bars of "Manhattan" with annotations that pertain to the small motives that make up the melody, beginning with motive "a," the "head motive," which consists, sensibly enough, of the notes that set the lyrics "We'll have Manhattan." This motive is distinguished both by the jaunty short-long-short rhythm that is so strongly associated with the song and by the two long notes at the end, which complete the key word "Manhattan." Thus, the motive has a distinctive melody and rhythmic shape, analogous to a well-shaped spoken phrase, and that of course is what Lorenz Hart has supplied, with "We'll have Manhattan."

Ex. 2-12. "Manhattan": Motives

At the beginning of bar 2 (Ex. 2-12) notice how important the silence is, signified by the notated rest. This separates head motive "a" from the melodic figures that follow it. The first of these, marked "a'," turns out to be a melodic variant on the rhythm of "a," hence the attached prime. Here Hart rhymes three-syllable "Manhattan" with the three syllables of "and Staten," preserving in this amusing way the grouping in threes that is so characteristic of this song and that derives from the key word "Manhattan." I also note that the rhymed word "Staten" occurs not at the end of a line, but in the middle, hence it is a clever instance of *internal rhyme*, described in chapter 1, where it was illustrated by an example from this very song. Indeed, in the lyrics for "Manhattan" Hart uses internal rhymes throughout, often creating chains of three rhyming syllables that occur within lines.

Threeness is, in fact, everywhere in this song. We hear it in the second motive of the opening music of "Manhattan," motive "b" (Ex. 2-12), which ends with the three repeated notes that set "Island too." I have included the tail of motive "a" as the beginning of motive "b," a dovetailing. The lyric "It's lovely going through" is then heard as a variant on motive "b," marked "b'," which has a prefix of three notes, before ending on the three repeated notes ("going through") associated with the shape of motive "b." Moreover, the arrival on "zoo" completes a chain of three rhyming words, two of which are end rhymes: "too," "through," and "zoo."

In bar 5, the last of the repeated notes of motive "b'" (on "through") is stretched out, quadrupled in duration, in fact, and becomes the headnote of the three-note figure, marked "c." Because of its long notes this motive differs strikingly from its predecessors "a" and "b." Again, however, threeness prevails in the three notes that compose the figure: Bb-D-Bb. Perceptive listeners will hear the Bb-D as a reference to the same notes in "Man-hat" as it first occurred in motive "a" in bar 1.

Be that as it may, the motives in the opening music of "Manhattan" saturate the song. To illustrate, Ex. 2-13 annotates the passage that begins in bar 12,

Ex. 2-13. *"Manhattan": More motives*

which completes the first section of the song. As indicated by the small letters, bars 12 and 13 contain the rhythmic shape of motive "b'," without its identifying repeated notes at the end. This figure, however, is enriched by the inclusion of an expanded form of the melodic beginning of motive "a," in which "the subway" corresponds to "We'll have the." Although the notes are not the same, the contour configuration and the intervals between the notes correspond. In bar 13 (Ex. 2-13) I have assigned a new label, "d," to the three notes at the end of this form of motive "b" ("charms us so"), since the large ascending leap is a distinctive new feature in the melody. Motive "d" then occurs twice at the end of the phrase, bars 15 and 16, completing a chain of three-syllable groupings that began with "The subway" in bar 12.

In these measures (bars 15 and 16), which end the first double period of the Refrain of "Manhattan," motive "b" plays a major expressive role. By repetition and by rhythmic foreshortening, the motives lend considerable momentum to the song and create a feeling of spontaneity that is appropriate to the joyful idea that its lyrics present.

The repetition of the four motives and their subtle combination are reflected in the ingenious rhymes, inner rhymes, and rhythms of the lyrics to produce a charming and lively musical panorama that must have generated the immediate appeal that Rodgers describes in the audience reaction to the first performance.

Rhythmic Performance Variables

In the sheet music versions of the song, which I am using for the examples, the rhythmic pattern of the lyrics of "Manhattan" almost always follows the fixed metrical plan, as Ex. 2-14a illustrates for bar 1 of the song. Here almost all four numbered metrical (quarter note) beats strictly correspond to notes and the natural accents of the lyrics.

Ex. 2-14. *"Manhattan": Swung rhythms*

In actual practice, however, performers alter the metrical rhythm of the notated version in Ex. 2-14 in various ways, one of which is shown in Ex. 2-14b. Comparing Ex. 2-14a with Ex. 2-14b, we see that a constant pattern of eighth-note triplets replaces the original dotted figure followed by two quarter notes. As a result, "-tan" of "Manhattan" comes in just before the metrical fourth beat, anticipating it by exactly one eighth note within an eighth-note triplet, a form of syncopation. Examples 2-4c and 2-4d represent a second instructive instance in "Manhattan": the notated rhythm of "Staten Island too" compared with a common way of varying that rhythm to produce a normal "swung" pattern. After "Staten" the syllables of the lyrics as shown in Ex. 2-14d fall exactly one eighth note sooner than the metrical beat pattern, as notated in Ex. 2-14c.

The notated rhythm of the sheet music of "Manhattan" was probably never performed exactly in that way by professional musicians, either in 1925 or later. By 1925 the influence of jazz was firmly in place, and performers would routinely replace the "square" notated rhythm with rhythmic variables to create a more attractive string of syncopations (anticipations). Because this practice was understood by music publishers, the printed sheet music continued to use a more or less normative notation, one that was simpler and one that would be more accessible to Aunt Nell or Uncle Charlie when they sat down at the upright piano to render the song, perhaps as a sing-along with other members of the family.

In the final analysis, what captivated the contemporary audiences who heard "Manhattan" and what continues to captivate modern audiences is Rodgers' inventive melodic and rhythmic shapes, in all their charming variety, combined with the virtuosic lyrics of Lorenz Hart, with their gentle irony and ingenious amalgamation of the sonic and the semantic. As a former resident of that sacred isle, I very much doubt that Manhattan's subway breezes were "balmy" in 1925, any more than they are today, but the triple alliteration "balmy breezes blow" is as memorable now as it was then. Nor were push carts "sweet" in that year, though the internal rhyming of "Street" and "sweet" creates a sweet and "wond'rous" image that is timeless.

■

GEORGE GERSHWIN, "HOW LONG HAS THIS BEEN GOING ON?"
Lyrics by Ira Gershwin
CD Track 3

LYRICS
Refrain
Chorus I
A

I could cry salty tears;
Where have I been all these years?

Ex. 2-15. "How Long Has This Been Going On?": Leadsheet

Little wow,
Tell me now:
How long has this been going on?

A'

There were chills up my spine,
And some thrills I can't define.
Listen sweet,
I repeat:
How long has this been going on?

B (Bridge)

Oh, I feel that I could melt;
Into Heaven I'm hurled!
I know how Columbus felt,
Finding another world!

Chorus 2

A

Kiss me once, then once more
What a dunce I was before.
What a break!
For Heaven's sake!
How long has this been going on?

On December 27, 1927, the Kern-Hammerstein musical *Show Boat* opened at the Ziegfeld Theatre in New York and ran for 575 performances. Based upon Edna Ferber's novel, this extraordinary production was to become a landmark in American musical theatre, combining thrilling spectacle with trenchant dramatic content. On Broadway in the same year were Irving Berlin's *Ziegfeld Follies of 1927*, the first version of Gershwin's *Strike Up The Band*, which closed during tryout, to be followed by *Funny Face*, a resounding success—not to mention Vincent Youmans' *Hit The Deck*, and the Rodgers & Hart musical, *A Connecticut Yankee*. All this activity made 1927 a banner year on Broadway, many of the songs from which live on as standards known to millions of Americans, among them "Ol' Man River," " 'S Wonderful," and "Thou Swell," by, respectively, Kern and Hammerstein, the Gershwins, and Rodgers and Hart.

America and Americans received their share of international recognition in 1927 when Charles Lindbergh flew solo from New York to Paris in 33 hours. At home, the average teacher's salary was $1,277, the average lawyer's $5,200. The movie *Wings*, starring "It" girl Clara Bow, would win the first Motion Picture Academy Award in 1928 for Best Picture. The famous Sacco-Vanzetti murder trial, which was also an international event, ended with the execution of both men on August 22. In another controversial decision, Gene Tunney defeated Jack Dempsey for the heavyweight boxing title. Among other international events of importance, Chiang Kai-Shek defeated warlords in strategic locations in China.

It was a good year for modern concert music, with U.S. performances of works by Copland, Varèse, Bartók, Sessions, and Ives, although Cleveland audiences reacted negatively to their orchestra's performances of works by Arnold Bax and Alexander Scriabin. Violinist Yehudi Menuhin, who became a beloved international figure in music, made his debut at age 10.

The Pulitzer Prize for drama was awarded for *The Bridge of San Luis Rey* by Hamden, Connecticut, resident Thornton Wilder, who later referred to his mansion in that town as "the house the bridge built." Other American writers in the public eye were Sinclair Lewis (*Elmer Gantry*), Booth Tarkington (*The Plutocrat*), and Ring Lardner (*The Story of a Wonder Man*).

In sports, Babe Ruth hit a record 60 home runs and the New York Yankees won a record 110 games. Johnny Weismuller (later Tarzan) swam 100 yards in 51 seconds. In tennis, Helen Wills won the Wimbledon Singles. All in all, 1927 was quite a good year in the U.S. of A., especially when viewed retrospectively from October 19, 1929, the onset of the Great Depression.

After it was dropped from the musical comedy *Funny Face* in 1927, "How Long Has This Been Going On?" then appeared in *Rosalie* a year later.[9] Ira Gershwin tells us that the song was included in *Rosalie* "because Ziegfeld (Florenz Ziegfeld, the famous Broadway entrepreneur) liked it."[10] As it turned out, Ziegfeld was right: "How Long Has This Been Going On?" was the only song from *Rosalie* that became famous, but that happened only when prominent singers Peggy Lee and Lee Wiley recorded it long after the show had closed. It is difficult to understand why the special qualities of this song took so long to be recognized. However that may be, in more recent times "How Long Has This Been Going On?" is performed often, and it has been recorded by many singers, notably by Ella Fitzgerald, who sang it with Nelson Riddle's orchestral arrangement.

In its theatrical context, "How Long Has This Been Going On?" is sung in response to a first kiss, and the lyrics express the sweet delight and wonderment of the singer at this rite of passage. As I will show, the beauty of the lyrics and melody extends to the topography of the song as well.

As is almost always the case, the lyrics have their own quasi-poetic organization even within the standard thirty-two-bar form. Here we have an instance of the "popular song form," which contains four large sections labeled AABA. The A sections consist of one two-line stanza followed by a three-line stanza. Thus, the asymmetrical five lines fit neatly into the very regular eight-bar phrases, with the last line repeating what Ira Gershwin would have called the "burthen": "How Long Has This Been Going On?"[11] I will refer to this as the title or title phrase.

The design of the AA section is innovative. If we now look at the music, Ex. 2-15, we see that each line of the lyrics occupies two bars of music, with short lines 3 and 4 counting as one. These lines introduce the new end rhymes "wow" and "now," in preparation for the *first* word in the song's title, "How." This is a beautiful touch and one that is very characteristic of Ira's subtle manipulations. Unfortunately, he did not explain "little wow," leaving its meaning open to speculation by future generations of scholars.

Moving along to the Bridge, section B, we see that its four lines form a unit with rhyme scheme *abab*, breaking the pattern of the previous repeated A sections. From the standpoint of syntax, the first three lines of the Bridge end in very potent verbs ("melt," "hurled," and "felt"), while the final line ends with the ecstatic noun "world," which neatly closes the rhetorical progression.

Lyrics and Rhythm

Ira Gershwin catches us off guard (Ex. 2-16) with his whimsical beginning line: "I could cry salty tears" set by the repeated short-long-longer rhythm. (What other kind of tears are there? Did they have salt-free tears in those days?) The second line, "Where have I been all these years?" begins with the insistent repeated quarter-note pattern for "Where have I been," after which the melody drops for the three notes that set "all these years" with the syncopated pattern that exactly matches the short-long-longer rhythm of "I could cry" and "salty tears."

Ex. 2-16. "How Long Has This Been Going On?": Rhythm

The third line of the lyrics, "Little wow, tell me now," repeats the three-note short-long-long rhythmic patterns of bars 1 and 2. Then, in a striking change of rhythm, the first part of the final line, "How long has this been," introduces the series of short-long jazz-derived patterns that blend into the final three-note syncopation of "going on," which was the first rhythm in the song. Thus, the entire rhythmic pattern of the opening music consists of only three elements: the syncopated and jaunty three-note pattern at the beginning and end, the insistent four-note group ("Where have I been") and the short-long succession that sets the beginning of the title phrase, "How long has this been." This economy of rhythm matches the economy of note (pitch) patterns.

Now to the note patterns of the melody, which share importance with the lyrics. It is difficult to imagine a melodic configuration more unlike that of the model ballad of the period. Consider, for example, the aria-like contours of the opening of Jerome Kern's famous song, "Smoke Gets in Your Eyes" (1933), which the melody traces as it ascends from low Eb on "They" to the higher Eb on "true," creating a romantic ambiance characteristic of the European operetta (Ex. 2-17).

They asked me how I knew My true love was true.

Ex. 2-17. "Smoke Gets In Your Eyes": Melodic contours

Gershwin's jazz-influenced melody, in contrast, is tensely laconic, even fragmentary, originating, as it must have, in an improvisation by George at the piano. To enter the interrogatory mode of the lyrics we might ask: How are these short melodic elements unified to become a whole, if, indeed, they are? An inventory of the notes of the melody provides a partial answer. The melody of the first three bars uses only two notes, D and E. Two new notes, G and A, enter in bar 4 on "all these years." Bar 6 ("tell me now how") brings back notes D and E, an octave lower, and the first part of bar 7 returns G and A, so that up to this point only four notes, D-E and G-A, are in play.

D   E   G   A
(I   Got Rhy - thm)

Ex. 2-18. "I Got Rhythm"

Ex.2-18 shows these notes arranged in pairs. It also shows that they form a pattern that is identical to the opening music of Gershwin's "I Got Rhythm," which, in 1927, was yet to be written! The inventory consisting of only four notes is enlarged in a significant way with the setting of "going on" at the end of bar 7 (Ex. 2-16). There the syllable "go" is sung on Bb, a "blue note," and the last note of the bar is the diatonicized twin of Bb, B-natural. If we regard the blue note as a special and transient embellishing note, the basic inventory of notes for the opening music of "How Long Has This Been Going On?" then consists of the five notes shown in Ex. 2-19. These notes form a "pentatonic," or five-note scale, with all that it suggests, and to connoisseurs of classic American popular song, it suggests a great deal. In the most immediate sense, it suggests a strong link to the American popular song tradition, through Stephen Foster (1826–64), the

(I - got - rhy - thm)

Ex. 2-19. "How Long Has This Been Going On?":
Pentatonic

composer of "Camptown Races," and beyond Stephen Foster to the folk and religious music of black Americans. The pentatonic scale, which is a component of so many American popular songs of the Gershwin era and not just the songs of Gershwin, is as American as apple pie.[12] Of course the pentatonic component does not always appear in simple scalar form. We see this in "How Long Has This Been Going On?" where the pentatonic appears gradually: first as the two two-note groups D-E and G-A, the "I Got Rhythm" portion. Only at the end of the section, with the entrance of the last note, B, do we have all the notes of the pentatonic scale.

Gershwin's presentation of the notes of the pentatonic in "How Long Has This Been Going On?" is enhanced by rhythm, by lyrics, and especially by the one basic component of the song I have not yet touched upon: harmony. Ex. 2-20 shows the two chords that support the initial notes, D and E of the pentatonic. It is these opening chords that must have attracted the attention of musicians when

1   2

Ex. 2-20. "How Long Has This
Been Going On?": Opening
chords

they first heard the song. They are really wonderful sonorities, often enhanced in various ways, as in our CD performance. The first chord represents state-of-the-art popular song harmony, vintage 1927, perhaps originating with Gershwin. The pungent effect of the second chord comes from the dissonant notes in its interior, while the top and bottom notes, D and E, remain in place. This second chord comes right out of European concert music, that of the early twentieth century in particular. It could (and does) occur in the music of Igor Stravinsky, but of course in quite a different musical context. And it is a hallmark of the music of Claude Debussy.

In addition, the harmonies of "How Long Has This Been Going On?" include one that is idiomatically American and that occurs twice, first in bar 4, setting "all these years," and again in the penultimate bar, setting "long has this been." (Ex. 2-15). By idiomatic I mean that the chord in question (C7) comes directly from the blues, as the first change of harmony. By 1927 this item was part of the stock-in-trade of the American popular song.

Similarly, the blue note Bb at the end of the period is de rigueur in the sexier songs of this period. In the best songs, of which "How Long Has This Been Going On?" is an exemplar, blue notes are not treated casually. Here Gershwin treats the first in this song in a very special way. If you refer to Ex. 2-15, you will find it notated as the Bb in bar 32 that sets the syllable "go" in "going," just as the melody approaches the end of the title's query. When the blue note Bb lifts to B ("on"), we sense an intensification of the interrogatory mode: the descending implication of Bb followed by A suddenly changes with the upward shift to B. What more perfect pairing of note and word? This abrupt melodic shift happens in only one place in the song. In the parallel location, at the end of the second period in bar 15, there is no B-natural; the melody moves directly downward from the blue Bb through A to come to rest on the tonic G.

Special Features of the Lyrics

With lyric poetry, the main interest normally lies in the semantic aspect of the words and only secondarily in the sonic, the actual sound of the words. In popular song lyrics—which may be poetic in many respects but, as I point out in later chapters, are usually not poetry—the sonic aspect may be much more important, just because the words are sung to actual musical pitches (notes). Please refer to Ex. 2-15 in connection with the following discussion. Like all fine lyricists of the "classic" period, Ira Gershwin was sensitive to pitch, and that sensitivity is clearly demonstrated in the first two bars of "How Long Has This Been Going On?" where the repeated notes of the two-note motive D-E correspond exactly to the alliterative c-sounds and t-sounds in "could cry" and "-ty tears."

Ira also worked carefully with the double rhyme scheme, the internal and end rhymes, so that "I" in "Where have I" matches "cry" in the first line in pitch as well as rhythmic placement. This rhyme scheme also supports the connection between the two-note figures involving different pitches. Thus, "Listen, sweet" in bar 13 on G and A matches "I repeat" on E and D, and the D-E succession of bar 1 is now reversed to E-D. Alliteration is everywhere, and always manipulated with strategic artistry. In the Bridge (bars 17 through 24) the inner-end rhyme pattern is not used, and the pattern of end rhymes is stretched out to an *abab* succession: "melt-hurled-felt-world," which is a wonderful way of creating in the text the contrasting musical ideas of the new section.

Ex.2-21 shows the eight-bar Bridge of "How Long Has This Been Going On?" The special B of bar 7 returns here at the very beginning of the Bridge and

Ex. 2-21. "How Long Has This Been Going On?": Bridge

is the pivotal melodic note over the first four-bar phrase, linking the key interrogatory idea of the song with the lyric of the middle section. "On?" of bar 7 becomes "Oh" of bar 17, creating a sonic connection as well as a pitch connection between the two remote moments.

This emphatic melodic B seems to be a significant factor in Gershwin's choice of the key of C major for the beginning of the Bridge. Ex. 2-22 gives the

Ex. 2-22. "How Long Has This Been Going On?":
C major seventh chord

melody and simplified chords for the opening line: "Oh, I feel that I could melt."
Setting B in the context of the C major seventh chord gives it a special aura, since
the major seventh chord was beginning to acquire a particular aesthetic value
about this time.[13] Certainly it shows up in many Gershwin songs, for example,
in "I've Got A Crush on You" and "Who Cares." Its apotheosis, however, would
have to await Cole Porter and his epic ballad "Night and Day" some five years
hence. Here in the Bridge of "How Long Has This Been Going On?" with these
exotic chords, Ira gives us his all, with the erotic lyric "Oh, I feel that I could melt;
into Heaven I'm hurled"—erotic for that time, that is. Contemporary listeners
did not need to call Dr. Freud to tell them what those lines implied.

Verse

Before leaving "How Long Has This Been Going On?" I would like to say a
few words about the Verse. Ex.2-23, which includes only the "he" version of
the lyrics, "panties," "aunties," and "Dante's," illustrates an ingenious series of

Ex. 2-23. "How Long Has This Been Going On?": Verse

rhymes. Other than Ira Gershwin, probably only Lorenz Hart could have found such ingeniously witty end-rhymes. The amusing and mock-serious lyrics also contain many clever inner rhymes, including tot/trotted, tell/Hell, find/blind, and especially those that associate with the key word, kiss: list/insisted/sisters/ kissing.

The long Verse begins with the melodic B of the Bridge and bar 7. Indeed, the first phrase is a kind of paraphrase, or even a parody, of the melody of the Bridge. Sequencing up to B minor in bar 5 brings into play an even more specific reference to the Bridge: bars 21–24 (Ex. 2-21). Remember that the Bridge was probably written after the refrain, since that was the Gershwins' usual custom. B minor is the only minor tonality in this song, and since this is a happy song, we must assume that the minor key is intended to project a mock-serious and ironic mood. It is here that the word "kissed" appears, the first reference to the key word of the song. A similar change from major to minor can be heard in the setting of "So, my dear, I swore," which has a major cast, followed by "Never, nevermore," and a return to the minor mode, definitely intended to be mock-serious.

I would be remiss if I neglected to mention Ira's two "learned" references in the verse of "How Long Has This Been Going On?": the first to Dante's *Divine Comedy*, the second to Poe's "The Raven" ("Nevermore"). He seemed to take great pleasure in these and in other ways mixing high-class and low-class elements. The title of the famous musical, *Of Thee I Sing, Baby*, is a perennially amusing instance of a mix of stilted speech with the vernacular.

■

COLE PORTER, "WHAT IS THIS THING CALLED LOVE?"
CD Track 4

LYRICS
Verse

I was a humdrum person,
Leading a life apart,
When love flew in through my window wide
And quickened my humdrum heart.
Love flew in through my window,
I was so happy then.
But after love had stayed a little while,
Love flew out again.

Ex. 2-24. "What Is This Thing Called Love?": Leadsheet

Refrain
Chorus I
A

What is this thing called love?
This funny thing called love?

A'

Just who can solve its mystery?
Why should it make a fool of me?

B (Bridge):

I saw you there one wonderful day.
You took my heart and threw it away.

A

That's why I ask the Lawd in heaven above,
What is this thing called love?

Cole Porter said that when he wrote this song he was inspired by a native dance in Marrakesh that was accompanied by Moroccan tom-toms. That remark has been perpetuated by literal minded critics over the years. It is more than likely that this narrative, perhaps conceived in a vein left over from Porter's days as a Yale undergraduate, was delivered tongue-in-cheek. However, the "hootchie-kootchie" accompaniment figure in the sheet music refrain suggests that someone, perhaps at the publisher's, took Porter's story seriously and tried to lend an exotic flavor to the music. In the 1929 musical *Wake Up and Dream*, the song was performed before a huge African idol to the accompaniment of a persistent tom-tom rhythm, suggesting that, like the publisher, the Broadway people had a rather hazy idea of African geography, if they wished to convey Cole Porter's atmospheric setting, that is.[14] Perhaps the American public had not yet completely recovered from the evocative 1926 movie, *The Son of the Sheik,* which starred Rudolph Valentino, so that any reference to the African continent would have served the commercial purpose.

Closer to home, however, and further confusing the locus of the song, is Porter's performance instruction at the beginning of the Refrain: "Slow (in the manner of a 'Blues')." The reference to blues becomes musically concrete in the very first bar of the Verse, where the lyric "humdrum" is set by a blue note (Bb on Ex. 2-25). Like all blue notes, this one lies outside the key and evokes the sound aura of the traditional blues. By Porter's time, these blues references had been fully integrated into the American popular song idiom, due, in no small part, to the songs of George Gershwin. Indeed, in the verse, this very blue note (Bb) is the headnote of the Refrain, setting the first two notes of the titular phrase: "What is" in "What is This Thing Called Love?"

The lyrics of the verse are charmingly humorous and rueful. "Humdrum" is the key word in the first four lines, occurring in the first and again in the fourth. The sonic quality of the word itself, with its rhyming syllables, no doubt inspired the very "square" rhythmic setting of the first line, "I was a humdrum person,"

Ex. 2-25. "What Is This Thing Called Love?": Verse

which is repeated for the second line, emphasizing the "humdrum" character of the singer before love appeared on the scene in the metaphorical guise of a bird. The alliteration, "window wide" cleverly matches the internal syllabic rhyme of "humdrum," illustrating the kind of sophisticated detail that earned Porter his reputation as a major lyricist.

Rhythm is again employed with subtlety, when the only syncopation in the verse (Ex. 2-25, bar 7) interrupts the very conventional rhythmic patterns to set "quickened." Perhaps this is the moment to touch upon the perennial question: "Which came first, the music or the words?" Since Porter was his own lyricist, there is evidence to suggest that he often (perhaps always) began with the lyrics, in contrast to the usual situation, in which the songwriter wrote the music, after which the lyricist provided the words. Certainly, the isolated rhythmic syncopation here in the Verse and its correspondence to the action word "quickened" suggests the chronological priority of text over music.

The lyrics of the second part of the sixteen-bar verse begin by repeating "Love flew in through my window," perhaps suggesting by this exact repetition that the singer's humdrum personality has not altogether vanished with the appearance of love! Notice, however, that the second part of the verse begins at a higher pitch level than the first part, reinforcing the feeling of optimism and joy the singer experiences now that love is on the scene. But this changes radically with the final lines of the Verse, "But after love had stayed a little while, Love flew out again." Exactly at this point the pitch level of the melody reverts to that of the humdrum beginning of the song, descending mournfully to the close. On its way down, the melody collects two more expressive blue notes. The first of these sets the lyric "while" (Ab), and the second (Eb), occurring twice, sets the syllables

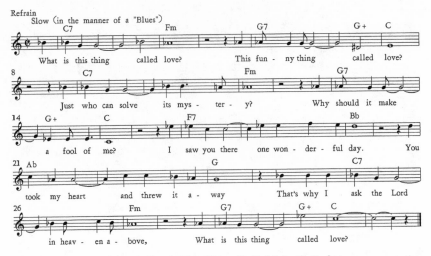

Ex. 2-26. "What Is This Thing Called Love?": Refrain

"out a-," just before the close. These three blue notes will return prominently in the Refrain.

As I observed earlier, the first of the blue notes in the Verse (B♭) now appears as the headnote of the Refrain, setting "What is." This very unusual beginning quickly became the hallmark of the song, attracting the virtually immediate attention of jazz performers and becoming a standard in their repertoire, where it remains today.[15]

At the end of the first period of the refrain (Ex. 2-26), the last word of the title, "love," which is always a special moment in a song, is accompanied by a minor harmony (F minor).[16] As a result, the listener has the impression that the entire phrase has a minor cast to it. This effect is intensified with the lyrics "This funny thing," as the melody continues downward. But as the phrase ends on "called love" there is a sudden and very striking reversal of the expected conclusion in minor. Instead of a minor chord (C minor), the phrase closes on a C *major* harmony, emphasizing the rhetorical question with an upward melodic gesture. At the same moment, the note that precedes the melodic note (C) that closes the phrase is, once again, the blue note (E♭/D♯) that we heard at the end of the verse, as described above in connection with the lyrics "out a -."[17]

The second eight-bar period of the Refrain of "What Is This Thing Called Love?" (Ex. 2-26) replicates the first period, but with some interesting differences. In place of the lyric "called love" we now hear, in the corresponding location in the music, "its mystery": three syllables replace the two syllables of the first. Because of the rhythm, the new lyric places the final syllable of "mystery," namely, "y," on an accented beat, thereby contradicting the accent pattern of normal speech. Although pedants have criticized this breach of good accentual manners, Porter knew what he was doing, for at the end of the next phrase the "y" in "mystery" rhymes "me," which is all the more effective for having been prepared by the shifted accent that brought the last syllable of "mystery" unexpectedly into the limelight. Actually, "me" preempts the spotlight here at the end of the second A section (bar 15) because the expressive blue note (E♭) precedes it, setting "a fool of." The second A section thus ends with a full close on the keynote (tonic) C, which is the only appearance of the song's nadir, intensifying its mood of dejection.

Moving along to the B section (the Bridge of "What Is This Thing Called Love?"), in bar 17 we hear a most remarkable event: the headnote of this section is our blue note (E♭) placed an octave higher![18] In fact, this note is the melodic apex of the song, conveying a feeling of joyful expectation as it is featured in the setting of "I saw you there one wonderful day." The semantic mood changes radically, however, with the next phrase, "You took my heart and threw it away." Porter has constructed this phrase beautifully, so that its descending contour matches perfectly the dejection depicted by the lyrics. Moreover, the notes that set the lyrics "You took my heart and threw it away" belong to the C minor scale, further intensifying the change of emotional mood. In fact, the entire Bridge is a very affective and memorable instance of musical word painting.

The lyrics of the final part of the song, the last section A, return to the rhetorical question presented as its title, invoking "the Lawd in heaven above," presumably to no avail. As a last resort, the final two notes, setting "called love," bring the blue E♭ into the same position it occupied as headnote of the Bridge, and the final keynote C is higher by a full octave. Some listeners may interpret this sudden raising of pitch at the end as a symbol of optimism, despite the lingering question embedded in the title.

■

ARTHUR SCHWARTZ,
"I GUESS I'LL HAVE TO CHANGE MY PLAN"
Lyrics by Howard Dietz
CD Track 5

LYRICS
Verse

I beheld her and was conquered at the start,
And placed her on a pedestal apart:

Ex. 2-27. "I Guess I'll Have To Change My Plan": Leadsheet

I planned the little hideaway
That we would share someday.
When I met her I unfolded all my dream,
And told her how she'd fit into my scheme
of what bliss is.
Then the blow came,
When she gave her name as "Missus."

Refrain

A:1–2 I guess I'll have to change my plan
B:3–4 I should have realized there'd be another man!

C:5–6 I overlooked that point completely
D:7–8 Until the big affair began;
A:9–10 Before I knew where I was at
E:11–12 I found myself upon the shelf and that was that.
F:13–14 I tried to reach the moon but when I got there,
G:15–16 All that I could get was the air,
A:17–18 My feet are back upon the ground
H:19–20 I've lost the one girl I found.

Due to his work as a producer of Broadway musicals (including his own 1948 hit, *Inside U.S.A.*) and as a music executive in Hollywood, the creative gifts of Arthur Schwartz (1900–1984) were not fully realized during his lifetime. Nevertheless, we have many fine songs from his pen, including the standards "Alone Together" (1932), the torrid "Dancing in the Dark" (1931), and the beautiful ballad, "If There is Someone Lovelier than You" (1932). The lyricist for all these songs was Howard Dietz, who also wrote the clever lyrics for the song under consideration here, "I Guess I'll Have to Change My Plan," from the 1929 revue, *The Little Show*.[19] Perhaps it is not inappropriate here to remark that a "revue" is to be distinguished from a "book musical," the latter based upon a plot (usually charming but flimsy), while the revue consists of a series of unrelated skits, some of which may be quite elaborate in plan, with miniplots, such as the one in which "I Guess I'll Have to Change My Plan" is embedded.

The setting for "I Guess I'll Have to Change My Plan," featured in *The Little Show*, is this: The singer (played in 1929 by the famous Broadway and movie actor Clifton Webb) has found out that the girl he has fallen in love with is already married. He then sings "I Guess I'll Have to Change My Plan." The actual change, which is not given in the song's lyrics, has a twist, however: he decides to pursue the loved one anyway, thus the happy character of the song, which contrasts with the mock-mournful lyrics.

Verse

This twist in the plot of the skit thus compounds the twist in the lyrics of the verse, where Dietz's ingenious and amusing near-rhyming of "bliss is" and "Missus" conveys the crux of the situation with appropriate irony. The audience is prepared for the shedding of "crocodile tears" in the forthcoming refrain by the supercilious lines, "And told her how she'd fit into my scheme/of what bliss is" (see Ex. 2-28).

The music at the end of the refrain reflects this quasi-dramatic situation

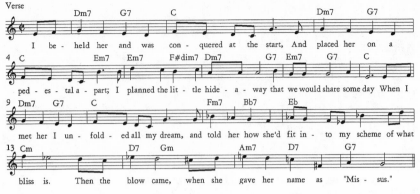

Ex. 2-28. *"I Guess I'll Have To Change My Plan": Verse*

beautifully, with the change to a minor harmony on "bliss is," further intensified by the change to yet another minor harmony of "blow came." These moments lead the listener to expect a close in a minor key (G minor). This expectation is frustrated, however, when the line "When she gave her name as 'Missus'" is accompanied by music that leads strongly and abruptly away from the expected close in minor to the *major* harmony that prepares the beginning of the Refrain.[20]

At other points in the Verse the harmonies are attractive and interesting, befitting Arthur Schwartz's status as a major songwriter of the era. A sudden change is immediately detectable with the lyrics "and told her how she'd fit into my scheme." This consists of an excursion to a distant harmonic area (with respect to the home key) that is completely congruent with the haughty tone conveyed by the words.

Rhythmically, the Verse observes the conventional and consciously "square" stereotypes. In this song, the stereotypes consist of repeated patterns of notes of the same rhythmic duration ("held her and was") followed by patterns that are exactly twice as fast ("conquered at the"). Only in the rhythmic setting of "bliss is" and "blow came," with their short-long values does the Verse break out of the square patterns of the earlier music.

Although the rhythmic patterns of the verse do not prepare the jaunty long-short rhythm of the opening melody of the Refrain ("guess I'll have to"), the descending contours of the Verse's melody do. Indeed, the falling unidirectional contour of the title phrase "I guess I'll have to change my plan" is one of the outstanding features of this song, and one that sets it apart from the many songs that begin with an ascending gesture (Ex. 2–29).

The second two-bar subphrase ("I should have realized there'd be another

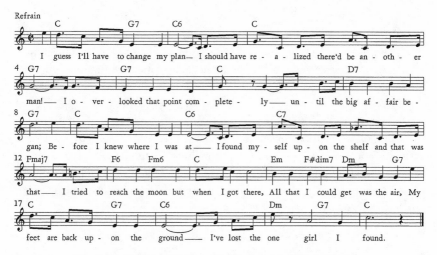

Ex. 2-29. "I Guess I'll Have To Change My Plan": Refrain

man") makes an abortive effort to ascend, but returns to the same three-note pattern each time. However—and this requires a little extra effort to hear and remember—the peak notes of each small ascending figure, beginning with "I should have re-," form a distinct pattern in themselves, which consists of the notes G-A-G. These fall on the syllables "re," "be," and "man." Why are the notes G and A important in this song? Because they originally occur prominently as A-G at the very end of the Verse, setting 'Missus.' They also occur almost at the end of the Refrain, setting "girl I" again as A-G. Whether this little motive signifies determination or resignation I leave to the reader to decide. Certainly its persistence enriches and enlivens the melody of the Refrain.

Even more interesting is the "mirror-like" design that underlies the first four bars of the melody. If the reader sings or hums (depending upon the audience's mood) the first five notes of the first two-bar phrase ("I guess I'll have to"), then the first five notes of the second two-bar phrase ("I should have realized there'd be"), this design should appear as if by magic. To make this design completely transparent, one more step is needed for the notes in the second phrase: arrange them in ascending order, beginning with the lowest note (C-D-E-G-A). Now, when the two patterns are compared, no further magic is required. Not only does the contour of Pattern 2 (ascending) reverse that of Pattern 1 (descending), but also the first three notes of Pattern 2 mirror—that is, reverse—the first three notes of Pattern 1, and the same applies to the last two notes of Pattern 2 with respect to the last two notes of Pattern 1. Complicated to describe, but easy to hear, *n'est-ce-pas?* To summarize this pattern:[21]

Pattern 1: E-D-C/A-G
Pattern 2: C-D-E/G-A

The scale on which both patterns are based is of course the ubiquitous five-note or pentatonic scale, which is endemic to the American popular song. Returning to the opening music just once more, I draw attention to the single note that was left out of the magical manipulations above, namely, the note (E) that sets "change my plan." This is the only note that is immediately repeated, and it is further set off by the rhythmic pattern, which consists of two notes of equal value followed by a longer note, without the "nonchalant" rhythm (a "dotted rhythm" because of the dotted note) of "guess I'll have to." Moreover, it is that centric E, placed eight notes (an octave) higher that sets "one" of "one girl" in bar 19 and qualifies as the melodic apex of the song.

Form and Residual Features

The form of this song is unusual in at least two ways. First, it is short: only twenty bars, as compared to the usual thirty-two. These twenty bars comprise five four-bar phrases, and each of the four-bar phrases is again divided into two subphrases, following the usual procedure for songs in this repertoire. Second, this short form exhibits a great deal of variety. The above display of the Refrain's lyrics, for example, provides letter names for each of the ten two-bar subphrases, indicating their distinctive melodic content. Remarkably, only subphrase A is repeated exactly. This is one way of showing what we experience when we hear the song: it is a fast-moving, energetic song, which strongly explains its sustained appeal since it first appeared on the scene in 1929.

Idioms in the Lyrics

Since they are not part of typical modern vocabulary, two colloquial items in the 1929 lyrics perhaps require explanation. The first of these is "upon the shelf," in the phrase "I found myself upon the shelf." To be placed upon the shelf means to be banished to a position of unimportance. The other phrase occurs in the line "All that I could get was the air." This does not mean that the individual received oxygen in some form. Usually occurring in the active form, as "to give someone the air," the phrase means to ignore, disregard, or, to use yet another idiom, to snub (to treat with contempt).[22]

Unlike the first set of lyrics, every line of this set rhymes. Following are the second set of lyrics for the Refrain:

I guess I'll have to change my plan
I should have realized there'd be another man!

Why did I buy those blue pajamas
Before the big affair began?
My boiling point is much too low
For me to try to be a fly Lothario!
I think I'll crawl right back and into my shell,
Dwelling in my personal H_ll.
I'll have to change my plan around
I've lost the one girl I found.

I refer to line C above of the Refrain of the first set, which ends with the un-rhymed word "completely." However, this second set contains some problematic moments. For example, the reference to "blue pajamas" was regarded as quite naughty at the time, and "I Guess I'll Have to Change My Plan" was sometimes called the "Blue Pajama" song. And the word in line 8 that rhymes with "shell" is discreetly spelled H_ll, with a humorous intention of course.

Finally, what does "fly Lothario" mean in line 6 of the second set of lyrics? The character Lothario comes from a 1703 play. Lothario, like Don Juan, was a seducer of women. Is a "fly Lothario" a womanizer who flees (flies) the scene when rejected? This is the most logical explanation I can find.

CHAPTER THREE
Songs from the Thirties

■

KAY SWIFT, "FINE AND DANDY"
Lyrics by Paul James
CD Track 6

Ex. 3-1. "Fine and Dandy": Leadsheet

LYRICS
Verse

Please forgive this platitude,
But I like your attitude.
You are just the kind
I've had in mind,
Never could find.
Honey, I'm so keen on you,
I could come to lean on you;
Honor and obey
Give you your way,
Do what you say.

Refrain
A

Gee, it's all fine and dandy,
Sugar Candy, when I've got you.

B

Then I only see the sunny side,
Even trouble has its funny side.

A

When you're gone, Sugar Candy,
I get lonesome, I get so blue.

C

When you're handy
It's fine and dandy,
But when you're gone what can I do?

In 1930, with the Great Depression in full force, President Herbert Hoover took an optimistic view: "While the crash only took place six months ago, I am convinced we have passed the worst." In this instance, the crystal ball was not merely clouded, but opaque. Nevertheless, life in the United States went on, demonstrating, once again, the resiliency of the American public. A few of the notable events of the year:

Astronomers identified the planet Pluto, completing the roster of Earth's known sisters. The first transcontinental commercial airline flights were established, and Babe Ruth hit 49 home runs. On the nutritional front, sliced bread was introduced by the folks at Wonder Bread, and in a burst of generosity the famous Chicago mobster-turned-philanthropist Al Capone opened a soup kitchen for destitute men.

In music, Ferde Grofé's "Grand Canyon Suite" became a semi-classical hit, while CBS began Sunday broadcasts of classical music played by the New York Philharmonic Orchestra. That architectural monument to art deco, the Chrysler Building, was erected in New York, soon to be followed by the apotheosis of that design aesthetic, Radio City, which was just in the planning stages in 1930.

The Motion Picture Academy award for Best Picture was given to Eric Remarque's antiwar drama, *All Quiet on the Western Front*, a reminder that World War I had ended only twelve years before. In contrast, the Gershwins' musical comedy satire on war, *Strike Up The Band*, was not a success. People apparently still took war seriously.

In this contemporaneous setting, the Kay Swift musical, *Fine and Dandy*, opened in New York on September 23, 1930, when Broadway was already feeling the effects of the national catastrophe. Nevertheless, in competition with the Gershwins' *Girl Crazy* (272 performances) and Cole Porter's *The New Yorkers* (168 performances), Kay Swift's *Fine and Dandy* sustained a successful run of 255 performances, establishing her as the first woman to compose a viable, full-length Broadway show.

Although the show has not been kept alive through revivals or by a movie version, the title song has remained a well-known item in the repertoire right up to the present time, with many recorded performances by a variety of artists. And Kay Swift (1907–1993) has remained an intriguing and provocative figure in the history of twentieth-century popular music, not only because of her own talent and achievements, but also because of her connection with George Gershwin, with whom she was closely involved as friend, collaborator, companion, and lover.[1]

The Other Songs of *Fine and Dandy*

In addition to the title song, two other songs from *Fine and Dandy* remain current: "Can This Be Love" and "Can't We Be Friends," the latter imported into the show from the 1929 musical, *The Little Show*.[2] Like many Broadway numbers the remaining songs of *Fine and Dandy* are fine and dandy in the context of the musical, but they did not transfer out of that context to become perennials. Among these I might mention three as characteristic: "Let's Go Eat Worms In The Garden" (containing the immortal lyrics "I love someone who don't love me, You love someone who don't love you. Let's go eat worms in the garden."); the attractive "The Jig-Hop," with lyrics reminiscent of Gershwin's "Fascinating Rhythm"; and "Nobody Breaks My Heart," a charming quasi-torch song with bluesy elements.

Unlike the professional songwriters who surrounded her in the New York musical theater environment, Kay Swift did not select a professional lyricist to provide the texts for the music of *Fine and Dandy*. Instead, she engaged her husband, James P. Warburg, whose calling was not to the world of Broadway but to the world of Wall Street, as his career was determined by his affiliation with the famous Warburg banking family. By reversing his first two names and omitting the last, Warburg produced his only published lyrics, those for *Fine and Dandy*, under the pseudonym Paul James. Despite his amateur status, Warburg produced lyrics that were often clever, usually skillfully contrived, and original — albeit with some rough moments in some of the songs. Those for the duets in the theme song "Fine and Dandy" are especially amusing, combining references to historical figures (Napoleon and Josephine) with mention of contemporary figures in the popular culture of 1930.[3]

Characteristics of the Verse

The Verse of "Fine and Dandy" gives only the slightest hint of the forthcoming Refrain. This consists not of a melodic-pitch motive but of the rhythmic pattern formed by the syncopation over the bar line in bars 3–4 that sets "platitude" (Ex. 3-2). The rhythm of "platitude" exactly matches the rhythm of "Gee, it's all" at the beginning of the Refrain. More sophisticated connections between Verse

Ex. 3-2. "Fine and Dandy":
Rhythmic motive

and Refrain, however, are lacking. In its unrelenting repetition of notes of the same duration (half notes) at the beginning, the Verse establishes its unequivocal membership in the genre "show tune," replete with clichés.

Indeed, the Verse is virtually a separate song. At the abrupt beginning of the Refrain the listener will perceive without great difficulty that the Verse has had its own key (C major), distinct from the new F major key of the Refrain. The Verse is also a complete song in another respect: it projects the typical thirty-two-bar form ABAC, in which each subsection occupies eight bars. (Section B begins with "You are just the kind"; Section C begins with "Honor and obey.") Despite its integrity as a complete song in itself, the Verse is almost never performed, at least by jazz musicians who have preserved this music in recordings and live performances. In general, singers have neglected "Fine and Dandy," so that the performance on the accompanying CD presents a rare opportunity to hear the music in its original form, complete with lyrics.

Characteristics of the Refrain

In its angularity and play on syncopations, the theme of the Refrain of "Fine and Dandy" is not vocal but instrumental in conception, reflecting Kay Swift's pianistic skill and keyboard orientation.[4] Over the first eight-bar period, the theme displays a very attractive rhythmic-melodic development (Ex. 3-3). During the

Ex. 3-3. "Fine and Dandy": Melodic ascent

first four bars the melody begins an ascent negotiating two two-bar phrases: "Gee, it's all" followed by "fine and dandy." In the second two-bar phrase a note is added to accommodate the "-dy" of "dandy." And in bar 6 still another note is added to the pattern on "when."

This rhythmic process of accretion provides a considerable degree of energy to the melodic line. In addition, the pitch pattern of the melody exhibits a corresponding development that propels the music forward to the end of the eight-bar period, with the lyric "when I've got you." This is shown in Ex. 3-4, where the series of little upward leaps are extracted from the entire melody to form the pattern *ababc*, beginning with "it's all," followed by "and dan-," repeated as "-ar can-," and finishing with the large leaps that set "when I've got you."

Ex. 3-4. "Fine and Dandy": Ascending leaps

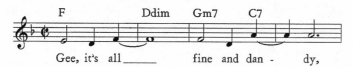

Ex. 3-5. "Fine and Dandy": Series of four chords

Harmonically, the first period of the Refrain of "Fine and Dandy" is relatively simple, consisting of a regular series of the four chords shown by the chord symbols in Ex. 3-5. Although it is the melodic and rhythmic design that makes the music move, there is an additional feature that supplies a distinctive character to the melody and gives it an impetus right at the outset: the headnote of the melody, E, which is scale degree 7 in the F major key of the song. This dissonant note resolves immediately to the next note of the melody, D, which then leaps to the third note of the melody to form the initial motive for the lyrics "Gee, it's all," a distinctive and memorable beginning for a famous song.

All these features no doubt made "Fine and Dandy" attractive to jazz musicians as soon as the music was heard and published and began to be transmitted in the usual way, that is, aurally. And, as I indicated above, it was jazz musicians, not singers, who established "Fine and Dandy" as a standard.

Form of "Fine and Dandy" and the B Section

"Fine and Dandy" is organized into a succession of eight-bar periods, creating an ABAC pattern that replicates that of the Verse, as discussed above. The first phrase of the B section begins with a reference to the head motive of the Refrain on "Then I on-." An abrupt change then occurs in the form of a contour reversal: instead of proceeding through a chain of ascending gestures as did the melody of the A section, the melody then plunges downward on "only see the sunny side," to end on D, the second note of the refrain and the nadir + 1, which is an ironic setting for "sunny side." The second phrase of the B section (bars 13–16) then repeats the entire descending pattern of the first phrase of the section—one step lower—to end on the true nadir of the Refrain, middle C, which sets "funny side."

Thus, section B of the Refrain offers a considerable contrast to section A. The same is true in the harmonic domain. Instead of the repeated succession of four chords we hear in A, the B section traverses the chain of fifths, as shown in Ex. 3-6.

F   Bb   Eb   Ab   C

Ex. 3-6. "Fine and Dandy": Chain of fifths

The C section of the Refrain of "Fine and Dandy" begins in bar 25 ("When you're handy") with a new harmony (Cm7), which signals the approach to closure. The "When you're handy" phrase leaps, via the down-up motivic contour of the very opening of the Refrain, to the apex of the song, D, a brief but special moment in the music. Following this, the down-up melodic contour persists until it breaks at bar 29 on "But when you're gone what can I do?" where it is replaced by the oscillating two-note figure (F-A). This figure will lead back to the repetition of the Refrain, with its multiple lyrics, to be picked up and repeated by D-F in bar 1. To emphasize closure and the special character of the final melodic gesture, it is only here at the end of the Refrain that the persistent syncopation over the bar line, so characteristic of the melody of "Fine and Dandy," ceases.

The charm and interest of the melody of "Fine and Dandy" reside in the ways in which its contour motives are developed and contrasted, its unrelenting drive through the regular succession of eight-bar periods, and the jazzy syncopations that characterize all the songs of Kay Swift's show.

On the compact disc, in response to a moment of inspiration, our artist, Richard Lalli, sings the parts of both Joe and Nancy. However, references in the text are only to the first set of lyrics as they appear at the beginning of the chapter and in Ex. 3-1.

∎

GEORGE GERSHWIN, "EMBRACEABLE YOU"
Lyrics by Ira Gershwin
CD Track 7

Ex. 3-7. "Embraceable You": Leadsheet

LYRICS
Verse

Dozens of girls would storm up;
I had to lock my door.

Somehow I couldn't warm up
To one before.
What was it that controlled me?
What kept my love-life lean?
My intuition told me
You'd come on the scene.
Lady, listen to the rhythm of my heartbeat,
And you'll get just what I mean.

Refrain
Chorus I
A

Embrace me, my sweet embraceable you!
Embrace me, you irreplaceable you!

B (Bridge)

Just one look at you,
My heart grew tipsy in me;
You and you alone
Bring out the gypsy in me!

Chorus 2
A

I love all the many charms about you;
Above all I want my arms about you.

C

Don't be a naughty baby,
Come to papa, come to papa do!
My sweet embraceable you.

"Embraceable You" was one of the hit songs of the Gershwins' *Girl Crazy*, which opened on Broadway October 14, 1930 (just about one year after the onset of the Great Depression), and ran for 272 performances. The show subsequently appeared in two movie versions and was featured in the very successful 1992 Broadway revision, retitled *Crazy for You*. The 1943 movie *Girl Crazy* attracted a large audience due in no small degree to its stars, Mickey Rooney and Judy Garland, and to the big band presence of Tommy Dorsey and His Orchestra.

"Embraceable You," introduced by Ginger Rogers, then a burgeoning star, and Allen Kearns, was no doubt the most popular song in *Girl Crazy*. But other songs in this great musical, which starred Ethel Merman, were also to become standards, notably, "Bidin' My Time," "But Not For Me," and the perennial "I Got Rhythm," which became a standard in the jazz repertoire. All these songs are performed and often recorded today, with "Embraceable You" still attracting special attention, just as it did at the time. It has been said that after 1930 this song was responsible for the consolidation of many love relationships.

Lyrics and Melody in the Refrain

The melody of the refrain begins with the three-syllable command, "Embrace me." This phrase repeats in bar 2, but then continues up one step, after which it drops suddenly to complete the line "My sweet embraceable you." What is remarkable here is Ira's four-syllable adjective, "embraceable," which of course became the key word in the title of the song. In Ira's usage some listeners may detect more than a touch of humor, a quality that offsets the imperative mode of the lyrics. This perception seems to me very appropriate in view of the original musical comedy setting, in which the characters who sing "Embraceable You" would be unlikely to use such long words in real life.[5]

After "embraceable," Ira ups the verbal ante by one syllable in the next line, with "irreplaceable," definitely a mouthful. Thus, the series 2-4-5 of syllable lengths in the opening of the refrain corresponds to the increase of tension of the vocal line: "em-brace," "em-brace-a-ble," "ir-re-place-a-ble." This linguistic succession contributes in the most natural way to the shape of the opening eight bars of music, with its gradual ascent from headnote E in bar 1 to D (on "-place") at bar 7. There is a certain inevitability about this ascending contour that derives from the repetition of the first four bars by the second four. The repetition, how-ever, is not simply one that involves the same notes. As summarized in Ex. 3-8,

Ex. 3-8. "Embraceable You": Melodic figures

the melody of the second four bars is a higher replica of the melody of the first four bars. The opening phrase in bar 1, labeled "a" ("Embrace me"), returns in bar 5 three scale degrees higher, beginning on A. This correspondence is indicated by the label "a′" attached to the bar 5 phrase. Similarly, bars 2 through 4 ("My sweet embraceable you") return in bars 6 through 8 ("You irreplaceable you"), again three scale degrees higher. In this way, the heightened rhetoric of the lyrics is reflected by the literal raising of the melodic figures. Moreover, the second four-bar phrase ends on the tonic or keynote, effecting a firm closure of the eight-bar (parallel) period and confirming the imperative rhetoric of the lyrics.

Formal Idiosyncrasies

Compared with that of the usual formal design of the popular song, the Bridge of "Embraceable You" comes in too soon—after the first eight-bar period, rather than after a double period of sixteen bars. This alone creates a sense of urgency in the song, but it is enhanced by the very sudden change to minor in bar 9.[6] The lover is restless! Sensitive as he always is to such musical changes, Ira moves from the imperative mode of the first period to a strikingly different lyrical idea ("Just one look at you . . ."), in which the lover's ardor is strongly expressed by the rhyming pair "tipsy" and "gypsy," words that suggest the abandonment of convention in the service of the overriding feelings produced by the onset of *l'amour*.

A beautiful touch here in the first part of the song (bars 1–16) is the alternation and balancing of the pronouns "you" and "me." Especially eloquent and passionate is the occurrence of "you" at the beginning and end of "You irreplaceable you." With the second part of the song, beginning in bar 17, "you" persists in the lyrics, and "me" changes to the possessive pronoun "my," which is definitely a sign of progress in the department of amatory relations.

By bar 17, when the opening melody returns, the imperative mode of the corresponding beginning music has vanished. Now we hear a straightforward declaration of love ("I love all the many charms about you"). The imperative mode returns in a playful way, however, with "Don't be a naughty baby." It is at this point in the song that an unexpected change occurs. If the second part of the song had duplicated the first, the Bridge, or something like it, would have reappeared here (bars 9–16). Instead, Gershwin composes entirely new music, beginning on the striking C major triad of bar 25 ("Don't be a"). This leads to the short (two-bar) phrase "Come to papa," which in turn introduces the consummate and climactic final phrase, "My sweet embraceable you," replicating the honeyed lyric of bars 2 and 3.

The following summarizes the form of "Embraceable You":

A	Bars 1–8	Opening section ("Embrace me")
B	Bars 9–16	Bridge ("Just one look at you")
A	Bars 17–24	Return of section A ("I love all")
C	Bars 25–32	Closing section ("naughty baby")

Bear in mind that this schematic summary does not fully emphasize the surprising aspects of the shape of this song, namely, the B section (Bridge), which, as remarked above, comes in "too soon," and the last section, C, which corresponds to it in the pattern ABAC. Melodically, section C does something very striking in the song: it reverses the pervasive ascending contour of the melody. We can hear this by comparing the melody of bar 6 with the melody of bars 25–26 at the beginning of section C (Ex. 3-9).

Ex. 3-9. *"Embraceable You": Contour reversal*

In bar 6 the ascending gesture, "You irreplace-" can be heard as two interlocking ascending figures, labeled "x" and "y," at "a"). At bar 25, these figures reverse and unfold, producing the descending line "Don't be a naughty baby." The resulting musical effect might be characterized in various ways. In perhaps the most discreet interpretation, this reversal of contour signals a motion toward closure, coming to rest on "Come to papa, come to papa do!"[7]

But the momentary cessation of motion on these repeated notes is interrupted by the final and definitive setting of the title phrase in bars 29 and 30. There, as shown in Ex. 3-10, the ascending melodic contour returns, to recall

Ex. 3-10. *"Embraceable You": Closing melody*

the beginning of the song as it sets the second phrase of the lyrics ("My sweet embraceable you"). This final motion is the expressive crux of the melody, rising to one of the special notes in the song, the apex E♭ (labeled with an asterisk) that underpins the second syllable of "embraceable." The melody then falls abruptly to close the phrase on the tonic note G that sets "you." Although most performers are sensitive to the final ascending gesture shown in Ex. 3-10, not all of them understand the crucial role the specific note E♭ serves: it is the expressive chromatic twin of the headnote of the entire melody, E, discussed in the following section.[8]

Special Notes in the Refrain

Of the several special notes in the refrain of "Embraceable You," I will mention only three. The first that captures our attention is the melodic headnote E, which sets the first syllable of "Embrace" (Ex. 3-7). In general, and not just in this song, this note occupies a special position in the tonic or keynote scale of G major, namely, the sixth scale degree.[9] In the melodic language of the American popular song this scale degree has several connotations. It is emblematic of the popular melodic idiom itself, which was developing at the time the song was written in 1930, since it is a nontraditional note on which to begin a melody and would not be found in that location, say, in the Lieder of Brahms.[10]

This note, scale degree 6, or E, in this instance, is normally committed to the note just below it in the scale (scale degree 5), so that the ascending trajectory ("Embrace me") elicits a feeling of unexpected tension, arriving abruptly, as it does, on the tonic or keynote, scale degree 1 (Ex. 3-11).

Ex. 3-11. "Embraceable You": Opening
on scale degree 6

The second melodic gesture, however, begins again on headnote E (scale degree 6), but continues the upward contour, moving past the tonic note to end on A ("brace-"). Immediately afterward the melody leaps down to scale degree 5 ("-a-ble you"), the note to which scale degree 6 normally belongs (Ex. 3-12). Thus, we must add D to our list of three special notes in this remarkable song.

If there is one note that attracts more attention than any other, however, it

My sweet em - brace - a -ble -you!
E . . .   . . . D

Ex. 3-12. "Embraceable You": Special notes

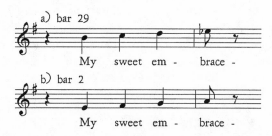

a) bar 29

My   sweet   em -   brace -

b) bar 2

My   sweet   em -   brace -

Ex. 3-13. "Embraceable You": Comparative
settings

is the high E♭ of bar 30 that sets the second syllable of "embraceable" in bar 30, which I have characterized as the expressive crux of "Embraceable You," shown above in Ex. 3-10. Compare the setting of "My sweet embrace-" in bar 2 (Ex. 3-13b) with the setting of the same text at the end of the song, in bar 29 (Ex. 3-13a) and notice the increase of intensity in the final occurrence. Not only is the final occurrence higher altogether, but it also rises to the apex note of the Refrain, that very E♭.

Dance Rhythms

The rhythmic patterns of "Embraceable You" are clearly evocative of the most popular ballroom dance step of the 1930s and earlier, the fox-trot. This is especially clear at the opening of the Refrain, where the melodic notes have the same duration ("Embrace me, My sweet embrace-"). At that point, the short notes and the syncopation of "brace-a-ble you" suggest a turn or other elaboration of the basic fox-trot step. The same regular alternation of the succession of equal durations and the pattern of short note followed by syncopation continues through the Bridge from bar 9, except that there the succession of equal durations is continuous, uninterrupted by rests, thus challenging terpsichorean imagination.[11]

Relation of Verse to Refrain

Like all the Gershwin Verses, the Verse of "Embraceable You" was written after the Refrain. The generalization implied by "all," although dangerous, is probably true.[12] Thus, it is always interesting and informative to consider the connections (if any!) between Verse and Refrain. For Gershwin the writing of the Verse very often seems to have been an opportunity for him to exercise his compositional skills. It is in the Verse that Gershwin displays aspects of his talent that place him above so many of his songwriting contemporaries. Let us consider just a few of these.

At first hearing, the Verse ("Dozens of girls would storm up") seems to have little to do with the melody of the Refrain. In contrast to the opening of the Refrain, with its short ascending gesture, the opening of the Verse presents a long descending contour (Ex. 3-14a). The headnote of the Verse is the ubiquitous

Ex. 3-14. *"Embraceable You": Descending gestures*

E, yet another instance of the special note discussed above. Although this E is higher by an octave than the headnote of the Refrain, octave-related notes generally are very close relatives in the tonal scale, other factors being equal. Why does Gershwin begin the Verse with this note precisely in this octave? I have just suggested one explanation: the high E, which is the headnote of the Verse, refers to the lower E, which is to be the headnote of the Refrain. A more important and subtler connection, however, has to do with the occurrence of high E♭ as the "expressive crux" at the end of the song, since that note is only a half-step away from the high E of the Verse and may, in fact, be regarded as its chromatic or half-step adjacency. To sensitive ears this seems a hyper-expressive version of E, one that derives from the key of G minor, the minor version of the G major key of the song.

An explicit and brief excursion into the G minor key does in fact occur in the startling gesture that accompanies "to one before" in bars 6–8 of the Verse (Ex.

3-7).[13] This strange figure is certainly intended to have humorous connotations congenial to Ira's hyperbolic lyrics. This ironic interpolation erupts right at the musical surface with the leap from E down to Bb, which creates the interval of the "tritone," familiar from classical instrumental music (and opera, as well). The intention is satirical, and Ira's superb intuitions grasp the opportunity for lyrical expression. In this gesture, the first and last notes are E ("to") and D ("fore"), respectively, foreshadowing the important occurrences of this note-pair in the Refrain.

At bar 11 of the Verse, shown in Ex. 3-14c, there occurs an unprepared change of key (to B major), a maneuver that is very typical of Verses in general. Gershwin fashions this change by purely melodic means, through a "chromaticized" version of the descending figure of bar 3, shown in Ex. 3-14b. The lyrics enhance this change through the interrogatory "What kept my love-life lean" with its triple alliteration.

Nonstandard Length of the Verse

As discussed earlier, the standard length of the Verse is sixteen bars. The additional four bars in the Verse of "Embraceable You" begin with the onomatopoeic rhythmic setting of "Lady, listen to the rhythm of my heartbeat" shown in Ex. 3-15.[14] Let us consider how this passage relates to the melody of the Refrain, which is about to begin.

Ex. 3-15. *"Embraceable You": Connections at end of Verse*

The repeated note B in the passage here at the end of the Verse (Ex. 3-15a) refers specifically to the B minor phrase in the Bridge of the Refrain in bars 9–10 ("Just one look at you"), shown in Ex. 3-15b, where the same note, B, occurs at the beginning of each bar. The connection is further strengthened by the association of "heartbeat" in the Verse passage with "heart" in the Refrain passage.

An even more explicit reference from Verse to Refrain involves the music that begins in bar 17 of the Verse (Ex. 3-15a) and the music near the end of the Refrain, in bar 27 (Ex. 3-15c). The repeated notes in both instances as well as the amatory semantic they share effect a strong connection between the two passages, even though they may be temporally remote when performed—less so if the Verse is sung *after* the Refrain.

These subtle correspondences between the melody of the Verse and that of the Refrain are wholly characteristic of Gershwin's songwriting and distinguish it from many of the songs of his contemporaries, in which the Verse may often be a completely distinct entity, charming in its own right, but without any musical connection to the Refrain of the song.

■

HAROLD ARLEN, "I'VE GOT THE WORLD ON A STRING"
Lyrics by Ted Koehler
CD Track 8

LYRICS
Verse

Merry month of May,
Sunny skies of blue,
Clouds have rolled away
And the sun peeps through,
May express happiness,
Joy you may define
In a thousand ways,
But a case like mine
Needs a "special phrase"
To reveal how I feel.

Refrain
Chorus I
A

I've got the world on a string,
Sittin' on a rainbow,

Ex. 3-16. "I've Got the World on a String": Leadsheet

Got the string around my finger,
What a world, what a life,
I'm in love!

A

I've got a song that I sing,
I can make the rain go,
Any time I move my finger,
Lucky me, can't you see,
I'm in love.

B (Bridge)

Life is a beautiful thing,
As long as I hold the string,
I'd be a silly so-and-so,
If I should ever let go.

Chorus 2
A'

I've got the world on a string,
Sittin' on a rainbow,
Got the string around my finger,
What a world, what a life,
I'm in love!

Harold Arlen wrote "I've Got the World on a String" for a revue produced at a famous Harlem nightclub, the Cotton Club, which was owned by individuals of questionable character and even more questionable activities. It featured black performers but served a virtually all-white and wealthy clientele that was attracted to the club by its excellent floor shows (revues) and its bootleg liquor, amply supplied by the proprietors.[15] Arlen and his lyricist Ted Koehler had been affiliated with this flourishing establishment since 1930, and several songs written for Cotton Club revues by Arlen and Koehler became published hits, among them "Between The Devil And The Deep Blue Sea" (1931), "I Gotta Right To Sing The Blues" (1932), the classic "Stormy Weather" (1933), and "As Long As I Live" (1934).

The mood of this joyous song stands in marked contrast to the situation that prevailed in the United States at the time it was composed and performed, a situation that affected almost everyone, excluding, perhaps, a select group that no doubt included the patrons of the Cotton Club and its proprietors. Still, in what can be seen in retrospect either as typically American optimism or as an obtuse failure to recognize realities, initiatives were taken that looked beyond the Great Depression to a happier future. One example is the 1932 opening of Radio City Music Hall in Rockefeller Center, which, with 6,200 seats, became the world's largest movie palace. And American humor did not go out of fashion with the Depression. In her first movie, *Night after Night* (1932), Hollywood sex symbol Mae West responded to the compliment "Goodness, what beautiful diamonds" with "Goodness had nothing to do with it." It is in this context that "I've Got the World on a String" earned a lasting position in American popular song as a symbol of humor, resilience, optimism, and the universality of human experience in the celebration of romantic love.

Although Ted Koehler's lyrics, both in this song and in others by Arlen, may lack the sophistication and refinement of, say, a Lorenz Hart or a Cole Porter, they represent a directness and make such clever use of vernacular phrases that they were and are attractive and memorable. The verse speaks of the need for a "special phrase," and that turns out to consist of the opening lines, "I've got the world on a string" and "Sittin' on a rainbow," where the vernacular contraction "sittin'" works perfectly with the long-short rhythm that pervades the melody of the song.[16] Even Cole Porter was not averse to using such vernacular expressions to achieve a joyously carefree effect in his lyrics, as in the title phrase of his song "Ridin' High" from the 1936 musical *Red, Hot and Blue*. Because of the ecstatic nature of the lyrics, we must excuse some loose syntactic ends here and there. For example, what is the subject of "may express," in the fifth line of the lyrics? Those who regard the posing of this question as an egregious instance of pedantry may well be justified. After all, "express" rhymes, internally, with "happiness," which is the main idea of the song. Who could ask for anything more, especially since the refrain contains such affective sonic connections as the alliterative chain that derives from the keyword "string": "sittin'," "song," "sing," and "silly so-and-so," not to mention the ingenious inner-rhyming "string" and "finger" and the charming remote correspondence of "rainbow" in line 2 and "rain go" in line 7.

And, perhaps the one feature that places Koehler's lyrics among the memorable of the period, in addition to the titular phrase itself, is the strategic delay of the kernel idea until the final line: "I'm in love." Thus, the *raison d'être* of the

What a   world, what a—— life,—— I'm in   love!————

Ex. 3-17. "I've Got the World on a String": Final phrase

title phrase "I've Got the World on a String" at the song's beginning occurs only at the very end of the first period and in corresponding locations twice more.

Of these, the final musical phrase, in which "I'm in love" occurs (Ex. 3-17) is itself a very special musical gesture in the song, for it begins with the alternation of two notes that have played special roles in the melody, and that now set "What a world, what a life." The first of these is the high F, which is the apex of the melody and which earlier in the song occurred only with the word "on" in "sittin' on a rainbow" (Ex. 3-16, bars 2 and 10), while the second note was the peak note D, decorated by E♭, in the opening theme, which occurs with the key word "world" in bars 1 and 25 and with "song" in bar 9 (Ex. 3-16). Moreover, a lower version of this crucial and idiomatic D (scale degree six) plays a key role in the phrases "What a world, what a life" (bars 5-6) and "Lucky me, can't you see" (bars 13-14). In the context of the entire song, then, the final phrase is built not from arbitrary notes, but from notes that have acquired particular semantic associations in the preceding lyrics. This renders the final setting of "I'm in love" in bars 30-31 (Ex. 3-17) all the more affective. Not only does it come right out of the F-D-F-D alternation of "What a world, what a life," but it also has a setting different from those of the two previous occurrences, now descending through the tonic chord as C-A-F, which emphasizes the very conclusive and definite rhetoric of those lyrics.

From the standpoint of rhythm, "I've Got the World on a String" is beautifully varied. The verse is restricted to a few simple figures and is totally lacking both in syncopation and in "swing eighths." The Refrain, on the other hand, features the "dotted" figure (eighth note followed by sixteenth, discussed in terms of the swing eighths) and the pictorial use of syncopation. This happens for the first time with the lyrics "move my finger" in bars 11-12 (Ex. 3-18), where "move

any   time   I move my fin -   ger,

Ex. 3-18. "I've Got the World on a String": Lyrics and rhythm

Ex. 3-19. "I've Got the World on a String": Bridge

my fin-" corresponds to the syncopated rhythmic figure that displaces the regular metrical pulse, depicting in rhythmic terms the motion described by the lyrics. Exactly the same rhythm occurs soon thereafter, setting "can't you see," lending a specific urgency to those lyrics and contrasting beautifully with the affirmative rhythmic pattern of "I'm in love," in which each note corresponds exactly to a pulse in the notated meter of the song.[17]

In the Bridge, which begins (as is usual in a thirty-two-bar song) in the bar 16 upbeat to bar 17, each two-bar phrase begins with the dotted figure and, except for bar 20, ends with a little syncopation over the bar line (Ex. 3-19). Melodically as well, the Bridge is quite "static." The same succession of notes in the same rhythmic pattern is heard three times: a series of A's followed by a long B, again with a small variation in bar 20. For the final two-bar phrase, however, the melody finally moves—down to a series of G's followed by the terminal A ("go") in bars 23-24. Thus, the melody of the Bridge consists of only three notes: A, B, and G! This creates quite a contrast with the hyperactive, instrumental melodic contours of the music surrounding the Bridge section. Why would Arlen write such a presumably static melody? Because the musical motion here is driven by *harmonic* change. The chord changes that unfold in the Bridge follow a traditional pattern, a chain-of-fifths pattern, that moves relentlessly toward the chord that reintroduces the theme of "I've Got the World on a String" in bar 24.[18]

■

VERNON DUKE, "AUTUMN IN NEW YORK"
Lyrics by Vernon Duke
CD Track 9

Ex. 3-20. "Autumn in New York": Leadsheet

LYRICS
Verse

It's time to end my lonely holiday
And bid the country a hasty farewell.
So on this gray and melancholy day
I'll move to a Manhattan hotel.
I'll dispose of my rose-colored chattels
And prepare for my share of adventures and battles
Here on the twenty-seventh floor,
Looking down on the city I hate and adore!

Refrain:
Chorus I
A

Autumn in New York
Why does it seem so inviting?
Autumn in New York
It spells the thrill of first nighting.

B (Bridge)

Glittering crowds and shimmering clouds
In canyons of steel,
They're making me feel
I'm home.

Chorus 2
A

It's Autumn in New York
That brings the promise of new love.
Autumn in New York
Is often mingled with pain.

C

Dreamers with empty hands
May sigh for exotic lands
It's Autumn in New York
It's good to live it again.

Prohibition of the public manufacture of alcoholic beverages had been established in 1919, through the Eighteenth Amendment to the Constitution. It was repealed in 1933 by the 21st Amendment, as everyone ultimately recognized that the law was effective only in the production of gangsters connected with the bootlegging industry. In 1934, the construction of cocktail lounges became a major part of the building industry.

As crime associated with bootlegging wound down, so did many of its stellar figures. John Dillinger (1902-34), bank robber and murderer extraordinaire (sixteen known killings), was shot to death by FBI agents in July as he left a movie theatre where he had just seen *Manhattan Melody*. Everyone loved the movies in those days. Folk figures "Baby Face" Nelson, "Pretty Boy" Floyd, and Bonnie and Clyde—later immortalized in a movie—also went to meet their maker, all under violent circumstances.

The Hays Office established a code of decency for the motion picture industry, including a ban on the depiction of double beds or naked babies, or any suggestion of seduction or of cohabitation without marriage. Unmarried Hollywood couples allegedly included Clark Gable and Carole Lombard, George Raft and Virginia Pine, and Robert Taylor and Barbara Stanwyck. As usual, American culture was riddled with contradictions.

The continuing erosion of soil in the plains states from dust storms was responsible for the increasing migration westward. This national tragedy and its consequences were later immortalized in John Steinbeck's 1939 Pulitzer Prize winning book, *The Grapes of Wrath*. Also on the national scene, the Social Security Act was passed, while unemployment was at 21.7%. A ticket to the Metropolitan Opera on a Saturday evening cost between $1.50 and $4.00, but the price of admission to a movie was between 35 and 50 cents. Movies flourished with such gems as Academy Award-winning *It Happened One Night* (starring Clark Gable and Claudette Colbert), *The Gay Divorcée* (Fred Astaire and Ginger Rogers), and *Of Human Bondage* (Leslie Howard and Bette Davis).

In popular music, the Big Band era was in full swing, literally, with Benny Goodman, Duke Ellington, Jimmy Lunceford, the Dorsey Brothers, and other fine groups. Song writers continued to produce wonderful melodies, such as "Blue Moon," by Rodgers and Hart, Harry Warren's "I Only Have Eyes For You," "You And The Night And The Music," by Arthur Schwartz and Howard Dietz, and Cole Porter's hits, "You're The Top" and "I Get A Kick Out Of You."

"Autumn in New York" appeared in the show *Thumbs Up*, which opened in New York December 27, 1934, and had 156 performances. It was Vernon Duke's only entry in this musical. He had been involved with American musical theater productions since 1925, but the first show for which he wrote all the music was *Walk A Little Faster* (1932), the musical that contained what is perhaps his most famous song, "April In Paris." Unfortunately, *Thumbs Up* was completely overshadowed by Cole Porter's *Anything Goes*, which had opened on November 21 of that year and ran for 420 performances. Among its songs were the hits "Anything Goes," "I Get A Kick Out Of You," and "You're The Top."

"Autumn in New York" is the sequel to "April in Paris"(1932), with E. Y. Harburg's beautiful lyrics, dubbed the most perfect popular song of its era by someone—perhaps by Duke himself, who was known to have a very high regard for his music. Other well-known songs by Vernon Duke include "I Can't Get Started," (Ira Gershwin lyrics), "What Is There To Say," lyrics by E. Y. Harburg, and "Taking a Chance on Love" (from *Cabin in the Sky*), with lyrics by John Latouche. It is somewhat surprising that Duke, having worked with these highly skilled professional lyricists, decided to write his own lyrics for "Autumn In New York"—with considerable success, it must be added.

After emigrating to the United States from Russia via France, Vernon Duke's career as a songwriter began in earnest when, at the suggestion of George Gershwin, he changed his name from the Russian Vladimir Dukelsky. Vladimir, however, did not disappear from the musical scene, but continued to write concert music of a modern cast, which never received much public exposure. In contrast, his adoption of the American popular song idiom and the popularity of his songs that ensued are extraordinary. In these respects he is sometimes compared to Kurt Weill, although, in my opinion, the Weill songs are less idiomatic, whatever their other virtues may be.

In Duke's autobiography (*Duke*, 1955), he depicts himself as a colorful and gregarious character who knew everyone and was on familiar terms with many famous figures, including his fellow Russian, Prokofiev. His somewhat tangential relation with George Gershwin is often mentioned now, especially because Duke was engaged in the completion of songs that Gershwin left unfinished at the time of his death in 1937. The extent of his involvement in this work is still disputed, but it seems clear, for example, that he completed the Verse of "Love Is Here To Stay."

After "April in Paris" (1932), perhaps Duke's most beautiful and highly original song is the one recorded by our artists, "Autumn in New York." Indeed, the title suggests that Duke thought the two songs to be closely associated. It is perhaps surprising that "Autumn In New York" was not popular when it first appeared. The reason for this seems apparent—to me, at least, for in terms of harmonic progression and melodic contour the song was years ahead of its time. It was not until the 1950s that "Autumn In New York" became a standard, and even then it was best known among jazz musicians, in large part because of Sarah

Vaughan's wonderfully expressive recording. It was never on "Your Hit Parade." With these observations in mind, I turn now to a discussion of those features of the song, which, like those of "April In Paris," set it apart from the mediocre songs of its era.

Verse

At the very beginning of the Verse, the little ascending gestures ("It's time to" and "end my lonely") are enclosed within a larger contour that descends, to end on the repeated notes that set "holiday" (Ex. 3-21). The second two-bar phrase then

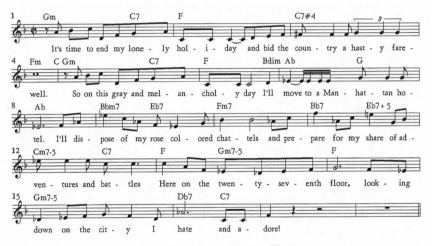

Ex. 3-21. "Autumn in New York": Verse

complements the first, ascending unidirectionally from that low C to the higher C that sets the syllable "-well" in bar 4. We will return to this phrasal pattern of descent-ascent in the Refrain, where it has a more specific connection with the lyrics.

The second four-bar phrase of the verse ("So on this gray and melancholy day") begins by repeating the opening of the first phrase, but shifts suddenly to a new harmony on "I'll move." In a beautifully pictorial way, the repeated notes of "move to a Man-" underscore the decisive tone of the text.[19]

In the second eight-bar phrase of the traditional sixteen-bar verse, the lyrics project a more optimistic mood, with the amusing inner rhyme "dispose" and "rose" and the witty introduction of the highfalutin word "chattels," in the fashion of Ira Gershwin.[20]

With its dramatically ascending and descending motions, the melody of this second part of the verse differs radically from that of the first, especially the ascent to the peak on "and prepare," which is followed by the slower descending-ascending motion that sets "Here on the twenty-seventh floor." This phrase also returns to the home key of F major, thus refocusing the music and settling the song in a more peaceful and reflective harmonic environment.

But the most effective lyrics of the Verse are yet to come: "looking down on the city I hate and adore!" There is an increase in dissonance as the melody reintroduces chromatic notes outside the F major key ("looking down on the city"), and especially with the pungent chord that sets "hate." [21] The contrast, harmonically, with the consonant tonic F harmony that sets the closing syllable "-dore" could hardly be stronger. [22]

Thus, the verse of "Autumn in New York," with its contrast of country and city, its imagery of the Manhattan landscape and the introspective reflections, is a powerfully expressive part of the song. As is the case with many of the better songs in this repertoire, it really should not be left out in performance, although it often is.

Refrain

Contour plays a basic role in the refrain as well as in the verse. The initial descending gesture that is identified with the melody of the song and that sets

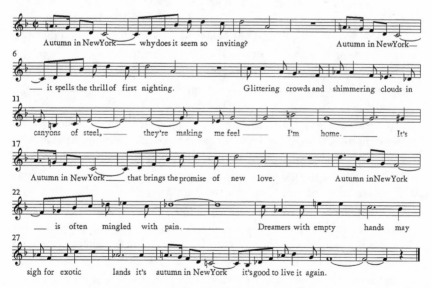

Ex. 3-22. "Autumn in New York": Refrain

the title phrase "Autumn in New York," is followed immediately by the contrasting dramatic ascent ("Why does it seem so"). These gestures immediately evoke images of the New York skyline, creating a stunningly pictorial gesture.[23] At the time Duke composed the song (1934), Manhattan's reputation as the home of the skyscraper was well established: At a height of 102 stories, the Empire State Building (1930-31) remained the tallest man-made structure in the world for many years, and it is still a mecca for visitors to the city.

The first two four-bar phrases of the Refrain are identical melodically, and both project the lyrics that express the attractiveness of the city, with "thrill of first nighting" answering the query "why does it seem so inviting?"[24] Each phrase ends with the expressive leap downward on long notes ("-viting" and "nighting"), although the harmonic setting for the leap at the end of the second phrase ("nighting") signals the marked contrast of harmonic orientation that begins to develop in the bars that follow. This part of the song begins with the descending gesture that sets "Glittering crowds," a new idea. The continuation, however, is accompanied by a harmonic peregrination very similar to the one we heard in the "rose-colored chattels" section of the verse.[25] Duke's lyrics here work very well with the change of key: the onomatopoeic "shimmering clouds," which contrasts strikingly with the image of "canyons of steel." "Steel" then rhymes with "feel" in the next line—a nice juxtaposition of words—and with the ever-active change of harmonic direction, the music arrives at the cadence, on the lyric "home."

Actually, however, the music has not yet reached home in the tonal sense of key, for the final section now begins with the return of the theme of the song and the title phrase, "It's Autumn in New York," to which is attached the optimistic "that brings the promise of new love." Melodically, this phrase is identical to the opening phrase of the refrain, so that "new love" receives the expressive descending leap associated in the opening music with "inviting" and "first nighting," unifying the two remote parts of the song.

Now, however, there is an unexpected change, and with it comes the most beautiful moment in the song. I refer to the setting of the lines "Autumn in New York/Is often mingled with pain." If the melody here had followed the pattern of the first eight-bar period of the Refrain, as described above, it would simply have repeated the first four-bar phrase. Instead, it begins at a higher pitch, with correspondingly greater tension. This tension does not diminish with the lyrics "is often mingled with pain." Now the melody carries the music to a minor harmony, setting "pain" in bar 23 (see Ex. 3-22). Nor is there a reduction of tension in the next lyrics, "Dreamers with empty hands." Although the music has now returned to the tonic key, it is the minor version of that key, F minor, that we hear. And it is at this point that the apex melodic note appears, the high E that sets the adjective "empty" in "empty hands."[26] Now the tension eases, with a return to a major harmony underpinning "may sigh for exotic lands." We are still in F minor territory, however, so that the sudden return to F major territory with the reappearance of the opening theme and title lyrics of the refrain in bar 29 is startling, an awakening of the "dreamers," as it were, and a trenchant instance of word painting. There is one more unexpected change yet to come, and that is the return to the minor key at the very end, after just one bar of the song's theme in its original form. Thus, the final line of the lyrics, "It's good to live it again," ends in F minor, the minor version of the tonic key, clearly concluding, in its plaintive way, with a less than joyful view of New York in the traditionally reflective and nostalgic season of the year—at least in American popular songs.[27]

In its harmonic development and its unexpected changes in particular, Vernon Duke's "Autumn in New York" is extraordinarily complex and, as I indicated above, ahead of its time by at least a decade. These features notwithstanding, or perhaps because of them, the song continues to appeal to both listener and performer.

∎

COLE PORTER, "I'VE GOT YOU UNDER MY SKIN"
Lyrics by Cole Porter
CD Track 10

LYRICS
Part I
A (AB): Double eight-bar period (1–16)

I've got you under my skin,
I've got you deep in the heart of me,
So deep in my heart,
You're really a part of me,
I've got you under my skin.

B (A'B'): Double eight-bar period (17–32)

I tried so not to give in,
I said to myself,
"This affair never will go so well."
But why should I try to resist
When, darling, I know so well
I've got you under my skin.

Ex. 3-23. "I've Got You Under My Skin": Leadsheet

Part II

C (AA): eight-bar period (33–40)

I'd sacrifice anything,
Come what might,
For the sake of having you near,
In spite of a warning voice

That comes in the night,
And repeats and repeats in my ear,

D (AB): eight-bar period (41–48)

"Don't you know, little fool,
You never can win,
Use your mentality,
Wake up to reality."

E (AB): eight-bar period (49–56)

But each time I do,
Just the thought of you
Makes me stop,
Before I begin,
'Cause I've got you under my skin.

Cole Porter's study in subcutaneous eroticism, "I've Got You Under My Skin," was composed for the 1936 movie musical *Born to Dance,* a wonderful extravaganza in the high Hollywood style, with glamorous sets, expert direction and camera work, and, above all, an all-star cast of performers: Frances Langford, a top singer; Buddy Ebsen, dancer and comedian who 26 years later was to star in the popular television series, *The Beverly Hillbillies*; the remarkable dancer Eleanor Powell; movie star James Stewart; actress Una Merkel, who in 1930 had starred in D. W. Griffith's *Abraham Lincoln*; and beloved comedian Sid Silvers. With this stellar cast it was not surprising that the movie was successful and that it was viewed by millions of Americans seeking respite from the Depression. In its initial appearance in the movie, Virginia Bruce, the sultry "other woman," sings the song to Jimmy Stewart, a handsome chief petty officer in the navy on liberty in New York. Stewart soon detached himself from such musical comedy roles and gained a reputation as a major dramatic actor.

Cole Porter's beautiful and passionate ballad appeared many times on "Your Hit Parade," the popular weekly radio show that featured songs judged to be current hits.[28] "I've Got You Under My Skin" appeared on the show on December 12, 1936, shortly after the release of the movie, and it occupied fourth place. It remained on "Your Hit Parade" for the next ten installments, falling to seventh place on January 30, 1937. However, the song reappeared much later, in tenth

place on October 8, 1966, when it was released by the Four Seasons, a male fal-
setto quartet, which apparently engaged the libido of a new generation in the
"if it feels good, do it" sixties. And Frank Sinatra kept the song alive before and
after that time. It was one of his standards, usually rendered energetically with
big band arrangements, and even included as part of his 1993 "Duets," on which
he sang it with Bono of the rock band U2.

In *Born to Dance*, "I've Got You Under My Skin" provides the music for
a dance routine by an anonymous team at the "Club Continental," which provided the ubiquitous nightclub setting so dear to Hollywood script writers. What
is noteworthy about this rendition is the Latin rhythm, which by this time had
become associated with much of Cole Porter's music, following the Latin American craze of the 1930s.

Given Porter's severe case of Francophilia, it is likely that the title was
suggested by the French idiom, "je t'ai dans la peau," which, rendered literally,
means "I have you in my skin." The lyrics of "I've Got You Under My Skin"
express passionate love with considerable daring, but they were not regarded as
offensive by the great American public, compared, say, with those by Lorenz Hart
in "Bewitched (Bothered and Bewildered)" (from *Pal Joey*), the stage lyrics for
which had to be excluded from the published sheet music lyrics.

"I've Got You Under My Skin" is a long song, spanning 56 bars, as shown in
Ex. 3-23. Since it was a movie song, it did not have to obey the constraints and
conventions of the Broadway theater, but rather could adjust to the more flex-
ible Hollywood cinematic script.[29] Accordingly, the lyrics are, well, longer than
usual. Also the rhyme scheme is looser than it is in Porter's shorter songs. In particular, many lines end with words that remain unrhymed: for example, "fool" in
"Don't you know, little fool" (bars 40–41), and "resist" in "But why should I try
to resist" (bars 24–26), lines that nonetheless contain the inner rhymes "why"
and "try." In short, Porter combines blank verse with traditional rhymed verse,
which, although not a novel procedure, is rather unusual in the popular song
idiom. He also uses direct repetitions to achieve special impact, as in the lines
that follow the titular phrase: "I've got you deep in the heart of me/So deep in my
heart, You're really a part of me." Repetitions of this kind of course come close to
the repetitive syntax of ordinary speech. Indeed, the verb "repeats" plays an important role in the lyrics in the line "And repeats and repeats in my ear" (Bridge,
bars 38–40), which itself repeats the word "repeats" on a repeated note (B♭).

At the same time, Porter uses traditional rhyming in eloquent ways. His strategic placement of words that rhyme the key word "skin" exemplifies this beautifully: "in," (also repeated internally) "win," (bar 43) and "begin" (bars 51–52).
The intricacy of the lyrics of "I've Got You Under My Skin" suggests that Porter

wrote them, at least in draft form, before he completed their melodic setting, a procedure that, as I mentioned before, reverses the usual arrangement involving songwriter and lyricist.[30]

Melody and Form

In approaching the melody of "I've Got You Under My Skin," I suggest that we begin by giving attention to its contour, in particular to the generally descending direction of the first two four-bar phrases. The second of these almost duplicates the first, except for the special treatment of the sentient lyrics "heart of me," where the melody dips down on "heart" and then returns to the adjacent note above for "of me." In the next four-bar phrase ("So deep in my heart/You're really a part of me") the melody continues its downward path, now very low in the vocal range (on middle C for female voice), then ascends briefly only to proceed downward again, reaching the nadir pitch of the song (B♭) in bar 15 on the keyword "skin," to complete its subcutaneous journey (Ex. 3-24). It is at this mo-

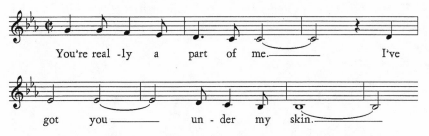

Ex. 3-24. "I've Got You Under My Skin": Melodic descent

ment that we realize we have experienced a large-scale musical painting of the text idea. What more potent way to project the idea of the song and the key words associated with it ("under" and "deep") than through this simple and pictorial topographical means?

Before discussing some of the melodic and harmonic highlights of "I've Got You Under My Skin," I would like to stay with its large-scale organization for a moment to consider the form of the song as a whole, which is outlined above with the lyrics. Essentially, this consists of not one, but two songs, designated Part I and Part II. Part I encompasses two eight-bar periods, A and B, which fill up thirty-two bars, exactly the dimensions of the conventional song. Part II, however, is an example of a "through-composed" song: each of its subparts has different music. Part II is twenty-four bars in length, just eight bars (one period) short of the thirty-two that would qualify it as a full-length song. It is true that Part II sounds

Ex. 3-25. *"I've Got You Under My Skin": Part II*

at first like a contrasting Bridge, with its repeated notes on "sacrifice anything, come what might" and again on "sake of having you near" (Ex. 3-25). There is never a full-fledged return to the opening music of the song, however. Instead, the final four-bar phrase is a version of the opening phrase of the song, projecting the titular lyrics. Thus, if Part II is a Bridge, it is a very long one. However one might describe this part, it seems clear that the overall form of "I've Got You Under My Skin" is as complex as it is affective and interesting.

The melody of "I've Got You Under My Skin," however, is not as complex when its motivic components are heard as guideposts that orient the listener, relating the various parts of the song. Two of these motives, which may be regarded as basic, are given right away. I refer to the three-note figure that sets "I've got you," which I will call the head motive, and the four-note figure that follows, setting the remainder of the line, "under my skin" (Ex. 3-26). These atomic com-

Ex. 3-26. *"I've Got You Under My Skin": Motives*

ponents, labeled "a" and "b" on Ex. 3-26, are distinguished from each other by contour and rhythm. They recur throughout the song, most often transformed in some clear way, providing the attentive listener with linkages that connect various moments in the song both sonically and semantically.

For instance, the ascending gesture of "heart of me" in bar 7 (Ex. 3-27) is heard as a contour replica of "I've got you," now altered rhythmically and trans-

Ex. 3-27. *"I've Got You Under My Skin": Motives*

posed down (seven semitones). The connection with the opening phrase is con-
firmed by motive "b," which *precedes* "a'" here in the second phrase of this refrain.

When motive "a," the opening or head motive ("I've got you"), returns for
the second time, at the end of bar 12 to complete the second eight-bar period, it
comes at a different location in the tonic scale and spans a smaller distance, the
shortest distance between notes in the scale, the half step (Ex. 3-28). This com-

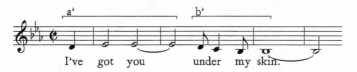

Ex. 3-28. "I've Got You Under My Skin": Motives

pression of the head motive of the song serves to intensify the final statement of
the title phrase at the end of the first section of the song. The compressed version
of "a," labeled a', serves an even more explicit expressive purpose when it sets the
beginning of the lyric "I said to myself" (Ex. 3-29). Here the second note of "a'" is
supported by a minor harmony, which enhances the semantic impact of "said to
myself." At the end of the phrase, however, on "go so well," motive "a'" coincides
with a return to the major tonic harmony, a more optimistic conclusion.

Ex. 3-29. "I've Got You Under My Skin": Motive a'

It is also in bar 21 (Ex. 3-29) that a third, and very simple, motive enters
the melodic scene, the repetition of a single pitch: "said to myself, 'this affair'."
Intensification by immediate repetition describes this rhetorical technique. We
hear it again in the next phrase, where it enters via a form of head motive "a," but
with a new harmonic setting of the lyrics "But why should I try to resist." And the
first section of Part II of the song, section C, is saturated with the repeated note
figure. Ex. 3-23 shows that this begins with the pitch F on "sacrifice" (bar 33),
moves up to the pitch B♭ on "sake" (bar 35), returns to F on "warning" (bar 37),
and again on B♭ at "-peats" (bar 39), and finally reaches the despondent and near-

climactic E♭ in bar 41 on "know, little fool," creating a remarkable ascending progression.[31]

In the preceding discussion I have concentrated on the head motive of "I've Got You Under My Skin" and its musical offspring. The second motive, motive "b," initially setting "under my skin" in bars 2–3, also contributes significantly to the unification of melodic structure in this song. Its closest relative, of course, appears when the same lyric closes the first double period, in bars 14–15 (Ex. 3-28). Here motive "b" has the same rhythm and descending contour as its original form, but is (obviously) at a lower pitch level and (perhaps not so obviously) traverses a slightly larger melodic span. Its final note, moreover, is one of the most important in the entire song, the nadir pitch (B♭). Remarkably, with the next occurrence of the "under my skin" lyric, at bars 30 and 31, the form of the motive, although very similar to that of its second occurrence, spans a still larger tonal space and is correspondingly more influential in the context of the song.

In sections C and D of Part II of "I've Got You Under My Skin," the "under my skin" motive "b" reverses, presenting an ascending contour to set "don't you know little fool" in bars 40 and 41 (Ex. 3-30).

"Don't you   know,   little   fool,

Ex. 3-30. "I've Got You Under My Skin": Reversal of b

But perhaps the most beautifully expressive occurrence of motive "b" follows the apex pitch F on "thought of you" in bar 50, as the motive, in its original contour, sets "makes me stop." It is at this moment that Porter introduces the brief silence, a notated rest, after "stop." This is a perfect musical gesture preceding the next line, "Before I begin," and of course it prepares "begin," the final rhyme of the key word of the song, "skin."

Of the additional occurrences of the "under my skin" motive in the song,

But each   time   I   do,   just the   thought of you   makes me   stop,

Ex. 3-31. "I've Got You Under My Skin": Bar 51 silence

perhaps the most immediately perceptible and memorable are the two adjacent forms in bars 44–47 that set "Use your mentality/Wake up to reality." Now the repeated-note motive is attached to the tail of the "under my skin" motive, where it provides emphasis for the imperative tone of the lyrics.

Finally, the striking and very unusual harmonic digression that occurs in the B section of Part I beginning at bar 25 deserves special attention (Ex. 3-32). This

Ex. 3-32. "I've Got You Under My Skin": Change of key

passage contains a very perceptible and abrupt change of key that sets the lyrics responding to the change of mood following the negative reflection, "This affair never will go so well." The new key and the progression that ensues give a special feeling to "But why should I try to resist when, darling, I know so well" and lead logically and inevitably to the return of the titular phrase "I've got you under my skin." As I indicated earlier, such motions that combine music and lyrics so perfectly lend credence to the assumption that Porter planned his songs and refined them with loving care.

■

IRVING BERLIN, "LET YOURSELF GO"
Lyrics by Irving Berlin
CD Track II (with "Change Partners" and
"Steppin' Out With My Baby")

LYRICS
Verse

1 As you listen to the band
2 Don't you get a bubble?
3 As you listen to them play
4 Don't you get a glow?
5 If you step out on the floor
6 You'll forget your trouble.
7 If you go into your dance
8 You'll forget your woe. So

Ex. 3-33. "Let Yourself Go": Leadsheet

Refrain

Chorus I

A

1 Come, get together.
2 Let the dance floor feel your leather.
3 Step as lively as a feather.
4 Let yourself go.

A

5 Come hit the timber
6 Loosen up and start to limber.
7 Can't you hear that hot marimba?
8 Let yourself go.

B (Bridge)

9 Let yourself go, relax and let yourself go.
10 Relax, you've got yourself tied up in a knot.
11 The night is cold, but the music's hot. So

Refrain
Chorus 2
A

12 Come, cuddle closer.
13 Don't you dare to answer, "No Sir."
14 Butcher, banker, clerk and grocer,
15 Let yourself go.

Irving Berlin wrote "Let Yourself Go" for the 1936 movie *Follow the Fleet*, in which Fred Astaire plays a happy-go-lucky sailor (this was five years before Pearl Harbor) and Ginger Rogers is a sexy night club entertainer. Ginger sings the song, backed up by the "girl trio," which was a staple of that era. Fred and Ginger then spontaneously execute an elaborate dance fantasy. It is *echt* and wonderful 1930s Hollywood.

Like those of all Berlin's songs, the lyrics are his, entirely his, I should emphasize, since it is well known that although he composed the melody, rhythm, and rudimentary harmony of his songs, he used the services of "musical secretaries" to arrange and notate the sheet music for engraving. Of course, professional arrangers orchestrated the music for the Broadway musicals and for the movies, which was the case for all the songwriters of the era and holds today as well.

The appearance of "Let Yourself Go" in a movie starring the beloved Fred and Ginger was certainly an important factor, perhaps the major factor, in the commercial success of the song. The Astaire recording first appeared on "Your Hit Parade" on March 7, 1936, in fifteenth place. By April 4 it was in third place, May 2 in ninth place, but finally fell back to fourteenth place on May 23. Altogether it was on "Your Hit Parade" eleven times.

Lyrics

The lyrics, which are intended to provide a setting for the snazzy dance routines, are mildly erotic, but stay well within the cinematically moral standards of the time.[32] They also represent Berlin's characteristically freewheeling style. The lyrics of the Verse, which is usually not performed, are not outstanding. In fact, they seem a bit forced. What does it mean to get a bubble?

The rhyme scheme of Chorus 1 of the Refrain is ingenious, consisting of three rhymed lines followed by the title phrase, which, when the four-line scheme is repeated, produces the pattern *aaa b ccc b*, which reduces to *abcb*.[33] One can detect the influence of Berlin's native New York City dialect in the series "timber, limber, and marimba," which he must have heard as "timbah," "limbah," and "marimbah," judging from the inclusion of the last item.[34]

The lyrics of the Bridge (lines 9–11) continue the emphasis on the imperative mode featured in this song, including even the repeated instruction "relax" in lines 9 and 10. However, the eccentric rhyming words "knot" and "hot," with "hot" carried over from "hot marimba" in line 7, maintain the central erotic focus of the lyrics, suggesting hot marimba, hot music, hot dancers, and so on. Connoisseurs of the sleazier portion of this repertoire will recall the colorful title from an earlier period, "I'm a Red-Hot Mama, But I've Got the Blues for You."

Finally, Chorus 2 presents the dénouement of the lyrics, couched alliteratively and seductively in line 12's "Come, cuddle closer," and giving quite a different semantic twist to the imperative *ritornello* phrase "Let yourself go."

Harmony

The alternation of major and minor features is so audibly apparent in this song that I hesitate even to mention it. The entire first phrase ("Come, get together. Let the dance floor feel your leather") is based on a single minor harmony (G minor). The next two bars serve as a connection to the two-bar title phrase, "Let yourself go," which is entirely within a single *major* harmony (G major). It is possible, perhaps even unavoidable, to interpret this dualism, which pervades Choruses 1 and 2 of the song, as the harmonic analogue of the initial imperatives (lines 1 through 3), set in the erotically persuasive minor mode, then followed by the hoped-for accession in major. It would seem that even the butcher, banker, clerk, and grocer among the moviegoers of the time would have detected the amorous undertones as well as overtones of the minor-major opposition in this song.

For the Bridge, Berlin has chosen a harmony that has strong blues associations, marked as the chord symbol C7 above bar 17 in Ex. 3-33. This is familiar as the first chord change in the traditional 12-bar blues. Since this chord occupies five of the eight bars of the Bridge, only three bars are left to negotiate a return to the key of G minor that begins Chorus 2 at bar 25. Instead of proceeding in an orderly fashion, however, Berlin sets the final three notes of the melody of the Bridge ("music's hot") with a remote harmony, E♭ minor. This leaves the return to G minor entirely up to the blue melodic embellishing note that sets "So" at the end of line 11, which may be a hot way to move from Bridge to Chorus 2, but it may resemble an aposiopesis to the listener. Be that as it may, the melody of Chorus 2 replicates exactly the first eight bars of Chorus 1, completing the uncomplicated textbook form of "Let Yourself Go" in the major mood phase of the minor-major dualism.

Melody

Should listeners not detect the amorous major-minor orientation of the harmony, Berlin also outfitted the melody with a provocative embellishing note, namely, the one that occurs on "get" in line 1 of the lyrics and then twice more in line 2 on "dance" and "feel" (see the asterisks in Ex. 3-34). This note (C♯) is a blue note in

Ex. 3-34. "Let Yourself Go": Embellishing notes

the minor form of the key of the song, G minor, and has a correspondingly jazzy feel. In lines 3 and 4 of the lyrics (bars 5–6 of Ex. 3-34), the embellishing note on "light-" and "as" performs a function similar to that of the first embellishing note and, like it, is also a blue note, now in G major. This proliferation of blue notes leads the ear to expect another one in the final two bars of the period, where the title phrase "Let yourself go" comes in (bars 6–7 of Ex. 3-34). Instead, however, the headnote of that phrase, B, certifies the first appearance of the major mode.[35]

Rhythm

Irving Berlin is usually not given full credit for one of the outstanding characteristics of his songs: their vibrant rhythms. For example, in his deployment of the four-pulse rhythm of the lyric "get together" (bar 2), only the first of the four pulses falls on a metrical beat; the syncopation is almost complete. The artistic use of long and short durations provides wonderful opportunities for dance interpretations, which were amply supplied by Fred Astaire in his choreography for *Follow the Fleet*. Again, we hear this at the very beginning of the song, where "Come" occupies an entire bar, followed in bar 2 by the energetic syncopation

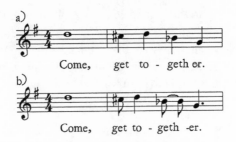

Ex. 3-35. "Let Yourself Go": Syncopation

of "get together." Examples 3-35a and 3-35b juxtapose the unsyncopated and syncopated notation of bar 2.[36]

Rhythm is also used in a pictorially terpsichorean way in "Steppin' Out With My Baby" (included in chapter 4) and in other songs by Berlin—especially in the movie songs, which *always* involve dancing. The Bridge offers a fine instance of this (Ex. 3-36). After the initial fast figure that sets "Let yourself go" in bar 17,

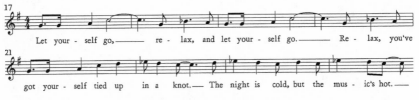

Ex. 3-36. "Let Yourself Go": Long notes

"go" receives a long note that extends into the next bar. This long note then links to the relatively relaxed setting of "relax," the second syllable of which occupies almost the rest of that bar. In Line 10 of the lyrics, "got yourself tied up in a knot," which follows, there is no such stretching of the rhythm, but instead a strong rhythmic impetus that culminates on the apex note (E♭) and the lyric "in a knot." It is refreshing to recall that in composing such refined associations as this, Berlin did not have to depend on the intuitions of a lyricist other than himself.

JEROME KERN, "THE WAY YOU LOOK TONIGHT"
Lyrics by Dorothy Fields
CD Track 12

Ex. 3-37. *"The Way You Look Tonight"*: Leadsheet

LYRICS
Refrain
Chorus I
A

Some day when I'm awf'ly low,
When the world is cold,
I will feel a glow just thinking of you
And the way you look tonight.

A

Oh, but you're lovely,
With your smile so warm,
And your cheek so soft,
There is nothing for me
but to love you,
Just the way you look tonight.

B (Bridge)

With each word your tenderness grows,
Tearing my fear apart,
And that laugh that wrinkles your nose
Touches my foolish heart.

Chorus 2

Lovely, never, never change,
Keep that breathless charm,
Won't you please arrange it,
'Cause I love you,
Just the way you look tonight
mm_mm_mm_mm_mm_
Just the way you look tonight

Jerome Kern wrote "The Way You Look Tonight" for the movie *Swing Time*, starring Fred Astaire and Ginger Rogers, a combination that alone would have guaranteed a hit. The RKO movie included two other very good Kern songs, "A Fine Romance" and "Pick Yourself Up," both comedic, but "The Way You Look Tonight," an ultraromantic ballad, quickly occupied the limelight. In the movie, Astaire, accompanying himself, sings the song to Rogers, while she is in the bathroom shampooing her hair. This creates an amusing situation when she emerges unexpected, shampoo and all, and he turns around to see her after singing a chorus. Times were simpler then.

Although *Swing Time* did not win the Motion Picture Academy Award for Best Picture of 1936 (*The Great Ziegfeld* did), "The Way You Look Tonight" won the award for Best Song, the first such award made by the Academy. Almost immediately thereafter, the song, which had been recorded by Fred Astaire, debuted in fifteenth place on "Your Hit Parade" on September 19, 1936. On

October 10 it rose to fourth place, then to second the next week, and in another week it took over first place, where it remained for six weeks.[37]

As perhaps everyone knows, "The Way You Look Tonight" is still going strong. For many years it was associated with Frank Sinatra, and of course it became a jazz standard right away. Still played by piano soloists and groups, it was a favorite of jazz musician Billy Tipton, whose revelation of dual identity gives a new semantic twist to the title of the song. Now it has become a standard for weddings and is sometimes seen on television soap operas. And pop music star Sir Elton John—no doubt inadvertently paying tribute—has incorporated the title in his song, "Something About The Way You Look Tonight."

All this attention notwithstanding, "The Way You Look Tonight" has retained its purity as a beautiful love song. For this we can thank both Kern and his extraordinary lyricist, Dorothy Fields. Kern is generally recognized as the father of the American musical theater song, and his output—the 113 shows (from 1904 to 1939) to which he contributed some or all of the music—remains unmatched. Of these, *Show Boat* (1927) surely occupies the pinnacle, both in Kern's *oeuvre* and in the American musical theater in general. Like many Broadway songwriters, Kern came to Hollywood during the Great Depression, seeking work when the New York scene became less active and Hollywood musicals had become significant vehicles of popular musical culture.

For many years, Kern was associated with virtuoso lyricists Otto Harbach and Oscar Hammerstein II, but with the move to Hollywood he changed his affiliations and began to work with the team of Jimmy McHugh and Dorothy Fields, especially with the latter. As a successful woman in this field, Dorothy Fields was virtually alone, but it is perhaps worth mentioning that credit for most of the lyrics bearing her name was shared with that of another lyricist, most often with Jimmy McHugh. She gained her reputation early in her career with such choice items as: "I Can't Give You Anything But Love (Baby)," which, although composed a year before the stock market crash, became a popular Depression song; "If My Friends Could See Me Now," revived some years later by Shirley MacLaine; and Jimmy McHugh's "On the Sunny Side of the Street (1930)," made famous by Louis Armstrong. Thus, by the time she began to work with Jerome Kern, Dorothy Fields was well established as one of the top lyricists, and her services were much in demand.[38]

Lyrics

With this background in mind, let us consider the lyrics of "The Way You Look Tonight."[39] First, however, we should note that there is no Verse, which is not unusual for Kern, especially in the movie songs. And, like many of the songs created in the superheated cinematic climate of Hollywood, it is a long song, extending to forty-four bars (without the repetition of the first part of the refrain), as shown in Ex. 3-37.

The form of the two outer parts of the song (Chorus 1 and Chorus 2) surrounding the Bridge is irregular. Instead of the usual double eight-bar period, summing to sixteen bars, here we have succession of three phrases, sometimes called a phrase group, the second of which is six bars in length: the normal four-bar phrase extends by appending the beautiful descending octave leap that sets "of you" in bars 9–10 (Ex. 3-37), which may be heard as an emotional expansion of the smaller opening thematic leap of the melody on "Some day" (bars 1–2).

Over the first three lines of the lyrics (Ex. 3-38) the words "low," "cold," and "glow" form a chain of rhyming words that enhances the forward motion of the

Ex. 3-38. *"The Way You Look Tonight": Bars 1–10*

melody and the encomiastic idea of the song. The semantic progression of the three words is very moving, from the two depressive words "low" and "cold" to the upbeat word "glow," which is followed immediately by the phrase "just thinking of you." As a further subtlety, notice the rhyming vowels in "Some" of bar 1 at the beginning of the song and "of" of bar 9 at the end of the extended six-bar phrase (Ex. 3-38). Remote rhymes other than end rhymes occur elsewhere in the lyrics, increasing their cohesion and long-range intensity. For example "day" in bar 1 clearly prepares "way" in the title phrase "and the way. . . ." in bar 11. Particularly beautiful in this respect is the pairing of "Love-ly" at the beginning of the second set of refrain lyrics with "love you" at the end of the second phrase in bar 10, which joins the poignantly expressive descending leaps (Ex. 3-38). In this second set of lyrics the chain now consists of the two adjectives that express positive feelings, "warm" and "soft" and the ever-sentient verb "love" in "love you."

In the lyrics of the Bridge of "The Way You Look Tonight" alliteration holds sway, with "tenderness" (bar 17), "tearing" (bar 19), and "touches" (bar 27). Remarkably, these three words begin with the consonant "t" sound, clearly related to "tonight" in the titular phrase. Thus, while "tonight" remains unrhymed in the lyrics, it is brought into the sonic network through the alliterative "t" sounds. The rhymed pairs in the Bridge include the charming "grows" and "nose," which refer back to the series "low," "cold," and "glow" of the opening music.

Fields repeats the "lovely" and "love you" association in Chorus 2 (bars 31–32 and 39–40) but introduces ostensibly new rhyme pairs, with "change" (bar 34) and "arrange" (bars 37–38). However, these vowel sounds refer back to "day" and "way" in Chorus 1. In short, she has created extraordinarily intricate and, yes, poetic lyrics, lyrics that I would compare with the best of Lorenz Hart's.

Rhythm

Rhythmically, "The Way You Look Tonight" is very conservative, not unusual in Kern's songs. There is no evidence of jazz influence, and syncopations are restricted to the Bridge and to notes that are tied across the bar line, as in bars 17–18, where "grows" enters on the last beat of bar 17 and is held over to the first beat of bar 18. The same metrical syncopation occurs with the rhyming lyric "nose" in bars 25 and 26. Elsewhere in the song, Kern adheres to the metrical pulses, a style that sometimes creates an impression of simple declamation. In the first four-bar phrase, for example, we hear two bars of whole notes followed by a full bar of quarter notes and ending with a whole note. Of course, singers, including the artist on our CD, will normally project these notated values with a certain degree of flexibility to avoid a very "square" interpretation.

Melodic Contour and Harmonic Progression

In the absence of rhythmic development that might advance the music in interesting ways, melodic contour and harmonic progression make the song move. After the initial descending leap on "Some day," a gesture often, as here, associated with the expression of a profound emotion, the melody begins a long ascent, broken periodically by a slight falling back. Thus, on "when I'm awf'ly low," the gesture ascends to Ab. The next gesture, on "When the world is cold," ascends one step higher, to Bb (on "world"), in the following we hear yet a higher motion (to C on "feel"), and then a rapid and unbroken ascent to the melodic apex of the song, Eb, which sets "of" in the first set of lyrics and the rhyming word "love" in the second. The phrase that contains the title, "and the way you look tonight," begins an ascending motion, but then falls back to the tonic Eb, on "look tonight," a gesture that sums up and closes the preceding melodic structure in a most beautiful way.

Ex. 3-39. "The Way You Look Tonight": Bridge

Bridge

The Bridge of "The Way You Look Tonight" begins on the same note as does Chorus 1, Bb (Ex. 3-39). The harmony, however, is radically different, projecting a feeling of "remoteness" that one often associates with this particular tonal relation.[40] Here the long-range contour is descending, in contrast with that of Chorus 1. However, this general direction is interrupted, dramatically, at bars 22 and 23, with the splitting of the syllables of "apart" by a large upward leap to the apex note of the song, Eb, which we previously heard setting "of" and "love" in bar 9. Once the melody arrives in this higher range it remains there for a moment, then unfolds downward through a sequential series of melodic figures (based on bar 18) until it reaches F in bar 30. On "foolish heart" the melody returns to the note that began the Bridge (Bb), the headnote of the melody of Chorus 2, which follows immediately as a replica of Chorus 1.

In Jerome Kern's "The Way You Look Tonight" we are again confronted with the issue of music versus word. Which mode of expression is the more powerful? Certainly Dorothy Fields's lyrics are virtually perfect, beautifully calibrated to the melody—even, I would claim—in her setting of the preposition "of" to the very exposed apex Eb in bar 9, a daring coupling that some would say violates a principle of text setting. In my opinion, however, this placement of the primary accent on the preposition accomplishes two goals: first, it liberates the phrase in which it occurs, "thinking of you," from the greeting card sentiment usually associated with it; and second, the word becomes aligned remotely with the inner-rhyming sacred word, "love," which then occurs in the same location as did "of" when the first period repeats, and, in an even more sensitive location, in bar 41 almost at the end of this beautiful song, in the phrase "'Cause I love you." In the presence of these beautifully crafted poetic lyrics, Kern's melody holds its own primarily, I feel, because of its extraordinarily simple trajectories. It is the melody that conforms to the lyrics, not the reverse.

■

IRVING BERLIN, "CHANGE PARTNERS"
Lyrics by Irving Berlin
CD Track II (with "Let Yourself Go" and "Steppin' Out With My Baby")

Ex. 3-40. *"Change Partners": Leadsheet*

LYRICS
Refrain
Chorus I
A (double period)

1 Must you dance ev'ry dance
2 With the same fortunate man?
3 You have danced with him since the music began.
4 Won't you change partners and dance with me?

A (repetition)

5 Must you dance quite so close
6 With your lips touching his face?

7 Can't you see I'm longing to be in his place?
8 Won't you change partners and dance with me?

Bridge

9 Ask him to sit this one out,
10 And while you're alone
11 I'll tell the waiter to tell him
12 He's wanted on the telephone.

Chorus 2

13 You've been locked in his arms
14 Ever since heaven knows when.
15 Won't you change partners, and then
16 You many never want to change partners again.

Irving Berlin wrote "Change Partners" in 1937 for the 1938 movie *Care-free*, which starred Fred Astaire as a psychoanalyst and Ginger Rogers as his flaky but sexy patient. Ralph Bellamy played her earnest and somewhat stuffy suitor. Apart from its starring actors, *Carefree* had very little to recommend it and was completely overshadowed by Frank Capra's *You Can't Take It With You*, which won the 1938 Motion Picture Academy Award for Best Picture, and by Disney's *Snow White and the Seven Dwarfs*, which captivated young children and their parents alike. In the same year Thornton Wilder, of Hamden, Connecticut, won the Pulitzer Prize for his play, "Our Town."[41]

"Change Partners" is the only hit song from *Carefree*, a show for which Berlin wrote all the music.[42] The song was on "Your Hit Parade" nine times, beginning October 1, 1938, and attained first place twice, strongly assisted by Fred Astaire's rendition of the song in the movie and by his subsequent recording. It would be difficult to overestimate Astaire's popularity both in North America and elsewhere at that time. By 1938 he was firmly established as a national hero, epitomizing American charm, good humor, insouciance, and resilience—all of which were attributes much admired during the Great Depression. Along with Clark Gable and Shirley Temple, Fred Astaire and Ginger Rogers were top box office stars as early as 1935.

Lyrics and Form

"Change Partners" is a long song, tailored for the ballroom scene in the movie, which has Fred dancing with another partner alongside Ginger and her partner

(Ralph Bellamy) while singing to her—and to the rest of the some forty couples on the floor. Not exactly normal ballroom etiquette. Ginger and Ralph respond by leaving the ballroom, whereupon something like that described in the lyrics takes place. I refer to this movie situation because the very specific narrative feature of the lyrics is unusual.

In length the song comprises fifty-six bars, consisting of a repeated double eight-bar period (thirty-two bars in itself), an eight-bar Bridge, and an abbreviated Chorus 2. Despite its unusual duration, the components of the song are conventional four-bar phrases, geared to the fox-trot contingent. Its smooth rhythms, the open spaces for turns and other maneuvers, and the virtual absence of syncopation identify the music as ballroom oriented, not as tap material for Fred and Ginger.

Characteristics of the Melody

The melody of "Change Partners" is so perfectly contoured that it could have been written by Jerome Kern. Its hallmark is the opening motion, a slow and sequential ascent that repeats the same rhythmic pattern on each step: "Must you dance—ev'ry dance—with the same" (Ex. 3-41). This is as clear a musical

Ex. 3-41. "Change Partners": Opening melody

depiction of the basic fox trot step as one might find in the dance music of the period. After its arrival on "same," the melody ascends rapidly, negotiating a new rhythmic figure (the triplet), to arrive on "man," the highest note thus far.

After the lead-in lyric "You have," the second eight-bar period begins on "danced" in bar 9 (Ex. 3-42). The note that sets "danced" (C) is strategically crucial to the melody, since it remains the highest note for a long stretch, yielding to the true melodic apex (E) only in bar 34 (Ex. 3-40), which sets the second syllable of "partners."

It is surely not happenstance that the temporary apex C in bar 9 lies exactly

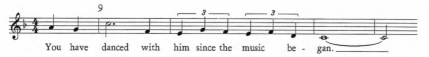

Ex. 3-42. "Change Partners": Temporary apex

eight notes (an octave) higher than the first note in the song, the nadir, so that the two Cs delimit the main span of the voice. Thus, in terms of its overall contour, the melody begins very low, gradually increasing in height and tension until it reaches the key word "danced" in bar 9. Berlin knew well how to capture the attention of the listener.

Most remarkably, the melodic phrase that follows "danced" in bar 9 (Ex. 3-43) descends rapidly to the very note, C, that began the song.

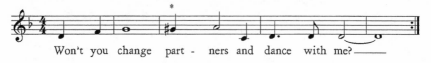

Won't you change part - ners and dance with me?_____

Ex. 3-43. "Change Partners": Chromatic

The title phrase is contained in the *ascending* gesture that follows: "Won't you change partners" (Ex. 3-43), and this key phrase is further distinguished by a completely new note in the melody (G♯) that sets the first syllable of "part-ners." Chorus 1 ends with a return to the first two notes of the melody (C and D) to complete the plaintive query with "and dance with me" in the very lowest register of the voice.

Bridge

At the end of the repetition of Chorus 1, in the second ending, the melody is on the tonic note, F, for "dance with me." The Bridge then begins in a new key (A♭ major), with the melody ascending rapidly through the notes of the A♭ chord to the strategic C that forms the upper boundary (Ex. 3-44). This note is decorated by notes that lie above and below it, then returns in bar 19 to set "you're alone." After repeating these motions the melody descends from that special C ("wanted on the telephone") in preparation for the onset of Chorus 2 at bar 25 (Ex. 3-40).

The melody of the first eight-bar period of Chorus 2 is identical to that of

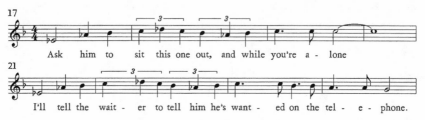

17
Ask   him   to   sit   this one out,   and while you're a - lone

21
I'll   tell the   wait - er   to tell   him he's want - ed on the tel - e - phone.

Ex. 3-44. "Change Partners": Bridge

Ex. 3-45. "Change Partners": Close

Chorus 1. However, with the arrival on the strategic C in the first bar of the second period (bar 33, Ex. 3-40), which sets the titular "change," a musical change is imminent. This takes place in the following bar where "partners" receives the special chromatic note (C♯) and the apex note of the song (E), as mentioned above. From here it is all downhill, as the lyrics suggest that the change may have more permanent consequences. In his rhythmic setting of line 16 of the lyrics Berlin seems unable to resist the temptation to introduce the only syncopations in the entire song to emphasize "never want to change," which of course is the clincher in the singer's lengthy plea to his beloved (Ex. 3-45). In the movie, Ginger Rogers leaves the scene in a huff at this point, whether out of anger or boredom with the plot is unclear!

■

HOAGY CARMICHAEL, "THE NEARNESS OF YOU"
Lyrics by Ned Washington
CD Track 13

LYRICS
Verse

Why do I just wither
And forget all resistance
When you and your magic pass by?
My heart's in a dither, dear,
When you're at a distance,
But when you are near, Oh my!

Refrain
Chorus I
A

It's not the pale moon that excites me,
That thrills and delights me.
Oh, no, it's just the nearness of you.

Ex. 3-46. "The Nearness of You": Leadsheet

A

It isn't your sweet conversation
That brings this sensation.
Oh, no, it's just the nearness of you.

B (Bridge)

When you're in my arms
And I feel you so close to me,
All my wildest dreams come true.

Chorus 2

A

I need no soft lights to enchant me

If you'll only grant me
The right to hold you ever so tight,

Extension

And to feel in the night
The nearness of you.

The year 1937, in which "The Nearness Of You" was written, saw many significant domestic and international events as the Great Depression intersected with European political turmoil and the threat of German military power. In the largest U.S. demonstration by organized labor, sit-down strikes closed General Motors plants. Howard Hughes flew across the United States in the amazing time of seven hours, twenty-eight minutes. British Prime Minister Neville Chamberlain appealed to Hitler for cooperation in keeping peace. In Wisconsin, spinach farmers erected a statue to Popeye.

The incomparable George Gershwin died unexpectedly in California on July 11, while his late songs ("Nice Work If You Can Get It," "A Foggy Day") became hits. Other famous 1937 songs include Cole Porter's "In The Still Of The Night," "Where or When" by Richard Rodgers and Lorenz Hart, and "September In The Rain," by Harry Warren. Much of American popular music, as was the case with other indigenous art forms, seemed untouched by world events. This generalization certainly applies to Carmichael's ballad, "The Nearness Of You," which is concerned with certain immediacies of love.

Hoagy Carmichael wrote "The Nearness Of You" in 1937 for the Paramount movie *Romance in the Dark* (released in 1938). After it was recorded by the Glenn Miller Band, with vocalist Ray Eberle, it began to appear on "Your Hit Parade," occupying eighth place four times. On the broadcast of September 14, 1940, it rose to seventh place, and then vanished from the program. It did not, however, vanish from public view, but continued to be performed. For instance, star vocalist Dinah Shore's recording of the song sold in the millions.

Carmichael's Career

Hoagy Carmichael's career had two aspects. One consisted of his work as songwriter and the other of his later movie career as actor-pianist. Born and raised in Bloomington, Indiana, in the heart of middle America and the home of venerable Indiana University, he entered and graduated from Indiana University Law School after a certain amount of indecision concerning a career in music. But he abandoned the legal profession when his first song, "Riverboat Shuffle," was published by Irving Mills and recorded by Red Nichols's famous jazz ensemble. From then on, he pursued a career as a songwriter and, later, also appeared in movies as himself.

As an actor Hoagy appeared in nine movies, from 1944 through 1956, which gained him a reputation as a genuine American folk character. Of his nine movies, the most important were *Best Years of Our Lives* (with Frederic March and Myrna Loy), released in 1946, a nostalgia-laden post–World War II epic, and *To Have and Have Not* (Humphrey Bogart, Lauren Bacall) in 1944. In the latter the famous song, "How Little We Know," was rendered by twenty-year-old Lauren, who was draped invitingly over the piano in a Martinique barroom while Hoagy tickled the ivories, shirt sleeves held in place by elastic bands, and cigarette dangling from his lip.

The published songs of Hoagy Carmichael include some 53 items. Of these, only a small number have contributed to the repertoire of classic American popular song. Two are included in the present volume: "The Nearness of You" and "How Little We Know." Carmichael's most famous song is undoubtedly "Stardust," from 1929, one of the all-time favorites, and together with several of the remaining songs—among them "Skylark," a very fine song—it continues to be recorded.

Form and Lyrics

Ned Washington, the talented Hollywood lyricist whose credits include Victor Young's 1932 "A Ghost Of A Chance" and Bronislav Kaper's 1947 "On Green Dolphin Street," wrote romantically erotic lyrics for Carmichael's elegant and basically simple melody, which contains only one note that lies outside the tonic scale of the key.

The form of the song is unusual because it unfolds over eight-bar phrases instead of the conventional four. Each eight-bar phrase corresponds to three lines of the lyrics, and those three lines are deployed in Chorus 1 according to the model established by the first eight-bar musical phrase, as shown below:

a It's not the pale moon that excites me, (two bars)
a that thrills and delights me. (two bars)
b Oh, no, It's just the nearness of you. (four bars)

The *aab* rhyme pattern created by the phrases of the lyrics, as displayed here, corresponds to the traditional bar form AAB. The two *a* lines are associated by "excites me" and "delights me," while the contrasting *b* line completes the thought, sensuously stretching out the response over four bars and expanding the rhythm for the setting of "nearness of you," the core poetic and amatory idea of the song. As I indicated above, the same design applies to the second eight-bar phrase. As a result, the chain of line-ending key words consists of "excites," "delights," "you," and "conversation," "sensation," and "you," so that "you" occupies the target position, which is certainly consonant with the idea of these sensual lyrics. In the song as a whole there are seven occurrences of "you" or associated words.

Bridge

In the Bridge (Ex. 3-47) Washington abandons rhyming lines and employs blank verse, placing "wildest" at the melodic apex on D in bar 21. The Bridge lyrics,

Ex. 3-47. *"The Nearness of You": Bridge*

however, end on "true," which rhymes remotely with "you" at the end of Chorus 1 and Chorus 2. Certainly the most interesting moment in the Bridge, apart from the climactic leap to "wildest" at bar 21, is in the line "and I feel you so close to me" (bars 18–19), where the melody skips down on "close to" and then moves just one melodic half step further to the only chromatic note in the song (Eb), which sets "me," creating a beautiful instance of word painting (Ex. 3-48).

The lyrics of Chorus 2 follow the pattern of those for Chorus 1, except that with "grant me the right" the second line runs on to the third syntactically, thus increasing the urgency and intensity of the song, which extends from that moment right to its end:

Ex. 3-48. *"The Nearness of You": Lyrics*

a I need no soft lights to enchant me (two bars)
a If you'll only grant me (two bars)
b The right to hold you ever so tight (four bars)
b And to feel in the night (two bars)
c The nearness of you. (two bars)

Indeed, this increase of intensity begins in earnest precisely in bar 32, normally the end of the typical song, where the additional two-bar line, rhyming "tight" in the previous line, begins an extension that delays the final appearance of the title phrase "the nearness of you."

Melody and Rhythm

The melodic-rhythmic organization of this final passage invites closer attention (Ex. 3-49). With the line "and to feel in the night" the melody rises to the apex D a second time, the first having occurred in bar 21 on "wildest" (Ex. 3-47). Now, however, there is an abrupt leap downward to D an octave lower, the only such dramatic leap in the song. The melody then changes direction to present the titular phrase in slower note values, in effect an expressively notated *ritardando*. What makes this final gesture so unusual is its relation to the setting of the repeated titular phrase throughout the song: It consists of the five notes that set "it's just the nearness" in Chorus 1 (Ex. 3-46, bars 6 and 14), which is a remarkable way of unifying the song in its final gesture.

Ex. 3-49. "The Nearness of You": Close

A Large-Scale Melodic Contour

However, the most memorable and initially appealing feature of "The Nearness of You" probably resides in the contours of the very first eight-bar phrase (Ex. 3-50). Over the short spans of the melody these contours begin with the ascending upbeat gesture that sets "It's not the pale moon." With the arrival on the highest note of this motion, C (setting "moon"), we begin to hear a slowly unfolding contour formed by notes that are not immediately adjacent. I have marked these notes by asterisks on Ex. 3-50. Each of these is introduced by a small leap from below, corresponding to the succession of lyrics: "pale moon," "-cites me,"

It's not the pale moon that ex - cites me, that thrills and de -
lights me. Oh, no —— it's just the near - ness of you.——

Ex. 3-50. "The Nearness of You": Descending contour

"thrills and," "-lights me." The peak notes of each of these small leaps form the
very audible descending stepwise contour C-B♭-A-G. At this point the pattern of
small ascending leaps breaks, and the next event is the large descending skip that
sets "Oh, no," the lyric that introduces the title, "it's just the nearness of you,"
with a new melodic and rhythmic figure. The striking descending skip on "Oh,
no" ends on the nadir pitch of the song, C, which is exactly an octave lower than
the higher C that set "moon" in bar 1. Carmichael exploits this relation by returning the melody to the higher C on "you" in bar 7, which then leaps down
the octave to the nadir C to begin the next eight-bar phrase on "It" in bar 8. This
phrase ends as shown in Ex. 3-51, where the tonic note F sets "you" in the title
phrase, effectively closing the melody of Chorus 1.

it's just the near - ness of you. ——

Ex. 3-51. "The Nearness of You": End of Chorus 1

Although large-scale contours such as the one Ex. 3-50 illustrates are by no
means unusual in the repertoire of classic American popular song, the instance
in Carmichael's "The Nearness Of You" is particularly salient.[43] The descending
stepwise line and the high and low Cs are also significant with respect to the text
setting, since they so clearly forge a connection between the traditional moon
image of bar 1 and the rhetorical "no" of bar 5.

Verse

Although at first encounter the Verse of "The Nearness of You" seems very simple
and straightforward, there is more to it than initially meets the ear. The ascending melodic contour, which resembles that of the opening phrase of the Refrain,

provides a clue. This two-bar melodic gesture begins on middle C and ends on the C an octave higher, just like the opening gesture of the Refrain. A bit more aural sleuthing reveals that the correspondence is even greater. This is shown in Ex. 3-52, where the lyrics at the opening of the Refrain are placed beneath the notes of the Verse to reveal that the opening melody of the Verse contains a slightly concealed replica of the opening phrase of the Refrain. Congratulations, Hoagy! A subtlety of this kind is more likely to be found in the Verses of George Gershwin.

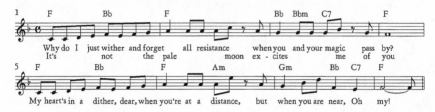

Ex. 3-52. "The Nearness of You": Verse

A second and beautifully expressive feature of the Verse is heard in the second four-bar phrase, with the setting of the lyric "distance" in bar 6. This leap, the first large leap in the melody, is a delicate instance of word painting, not only because of the leap, but because its second note, E, is the apex of the entire song, lying one step higher than the apex D of the Refrain (Ex. 3-47, bar 21, on "wildest"). Thus, the very short Verse, which is half the length of the traditional Verse, has very special features, features that relate it directly to the music of the Refrain, foreshadowing the opening music.

■

RICHARD RODGERS, "I DIDN'T KNOW WHAT TIME IT WAS"
Lyrics by Lorenz Hart
CD Track 14

LYRICS
Verse

Once I was young, yesterday, it seems,
Danced with Jill and Sue
And dreamed some other dreams.
Once I was young, but never was naive,

Ex. 3-53. "I Didn't Know What Time It Was": Leadsheet

I thought I had a trick or two up
My imaginary sleeve.
And now I know I was naive!

Refrain
Chorus I
A

I didn't know what time it was,
Then I met you.
Oh, what a lovely time it was,
How sublime it was, too!

A'

I didn't know what day it was.
You held my hand,
Warm like the month of May it was
And I'll say it was grand.

B (Bridge)

Grand to be alive,
to be young, to be mad, to be yours alone!
Grand to see your face,
feel your touch, hear your voice say I'm all
your own!

Chorus 2
A

I didn't know what year it was.
Life was no prize.
I wanted love and here it was
Shining out of your eyes.

Extension

I'm wise and I know what time it is now

    This wonderful song, now a standard in the classic repertoire of American popular song, debuted at the opening of *Too Many Girls* on October 18, 1939, at the Imperial Theater in New York. Of the star performers in this college football musical, only Desi Arnaz (husband of Lucille Ball, who appeared in the movie version) and comedian Eddie Bracken later attained broader recognition through movies and radio.
    "I Didn't Know What Time It Was" is not the only song from *Too Many Girls* that came to occupy a stellar position in the standard repertoire of American popular song. The show also included the very touching ballad, "You're Nearer," the poetic lyrics for which are regarded by experts as among the best of Lorenz Hart's many perfect lyrical utterances. "I Didn't Know What Time It Was," however, is distinguished by very special attributes, including time imagery and musical-spatial corollaries, which I will discuss briefly below.[44]
    "I Didn't Know What Time It Was," recorded by Benny Goodman, with

vocalist Peggy Lee, turned up in eighth place on "Your Hit Parade" at the end of November 1939, and stayed on in sixth, seventh, and eighth places through January 6, 1940, before vanishing. One reason for this abrupt disappearance was that many of the good songs of 1939—and there were many of them—were eclipsed by those that Harold Arlen and Yip Harburg wrote for the Technicolor extravaganza, *The Wizard of Oz*, especially "Over The Rainbow," unforgettably rendered by Judy Garland. And there were many other remarkable songs from that year, among them Jerome Kern's hyper-romantic "All The Things You Are" and Cole Porter's timeless ballad, "I Concentrate On You."

Although the year 1939 was a great one for American popular song, it was not a good year in the history of the world. After German troops invaded Czechoslovakia, Britain and France declared war on Germany, thus formally initiating World War II in Europe. The civil war in Spain effectively ended with General Franco firmly in place as dictator, and the United States recalled its ambassador from Germany, a symbolic act that foreshadowed complete U.S. involvement some two years later following the Japanese attack on Pearl Harbor, December 7, 1941.

In contrast to these horrendous international events—and driven by all the machinery of the gigantic recording industry, the traditional musical theater of Broadway, the vibrant movies, and the live performances of the big bands that serviced the ballroom dancing craze of the era—the American popular song moved blithely forward, seemingly impervious to the realities of the international scene, just as it had in the days of the Great Depression, the effects of which were even now, ten years later, still evident.

Looking back on these complex and tragic human events, it is absolutely incredible that a significant part of the American public could still respond to a beautiful love song such as "I Didn't Know What Time It Was." Of course by 1939 not only musical theater patrons but also radio and movie audiences had become accustomed to songs of high quality, and although they may not have been fully aware of the attributes of these songs, they certainly found them memorable and affective, just as we do today, when, with the advantage of perspective, we are able to view the creation of the entire popular song repertoire during this period as an extraordinary musical event. With these social and political events in the background, I turn now to the lyrics of the Rodgers and Hart ballad, "I Didn't Know What Time It Was."

Lyrics

The lyrics exhibit certain unusual features which I will mention briefly. For one, and characteristic of many later songs in the repertoire, there are many unrhymed words. For example, "Sue" at the end of line 2 in the Verse remains un-rhymed, as does "up" three lines later, which gives the verse a conversational, perhaps even a juvenile, quality that matches the singer's admission of naïveté, adroitly preparing the first and title line of the Refrain: "I didn't know what time it was." ("I didn't know what rhyme it was"?)

Not quite so unusual, but still of special interest, is the final line of the lyrics, "I'm wise and I know what time it is now." This ten-syllable line, which summarizes the idea of the lyrics, stabilizing their rhapsodic litany of love, accompanies the four-bar concluding phrase that extends beyond the formulaic thirty-two and thus creates a somewhat unusual length.

Otherwise the lyrics display the artistic virtuosity that connoisseurs have come to expect from Lorenz Hart. In the Refrain, we hear the alliterative chains: young, yesterday, and never, naive, know, now. And again at the end of the Refrain, the beautiful succession life, prize, shin(e), wise, time, a chain so meticulously constructed that the final word is the key word of the entire song.

The lyrics of the Bridge exploit the "list" technique, sometimes associated with the lyrics of Cole Porter, a very intense, rapid-fire succession of verbal phrases that list various qualities or attributes. In the first four-bar phrase, following "Grand," we hear attributes that the lover ascribes to himself or herself, while in the second four-bar phrase the lover lists the specific romantic actions that ought to ensue from the list of attributes laid out in the previous phrase.

> Grand
> to be alive, to be young, to be mad, to be yours alone!
> Grand
> to see your face,
> feel your touch, hear your voice say I'm all your own!

Rhyme plays a secondary role here in the lyrics of the Bridge: "alone" and "own" at the end of each long line are the only rhyming words.

The main part of the Refrain, moreover, exploits neither rhyme, near-rhyme, nor alliteration, but word *repetition* to produce its emotional effect. Again, the key word "time" occurs in lines one and three, along with the key phrase "I didn't know." And through repetition Hart gives special emphasis to "grand," introducing it just before the Bridge with the rhyming word "hand" (rendered tactile by "warm like the month of May"), then repeating it twice more, beginning with the first line of the Bridge: "Grand to be alive." In this strategic line the word "alive" forms a near-rhyme, albeit a remote one, with "time," by this point in the song established as the lyrics' most evocative word.

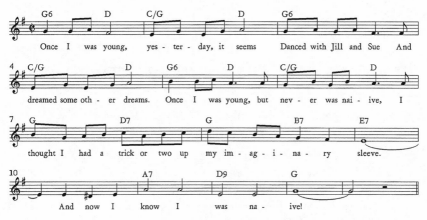

Ex. 3-54. "I Didn't Know What Time It Was": Verse

Harmony and Melodic Contour

In "I Didn't Know What Time It Was" there is a considerable amount of what might loosely be called "harmonic wandering" in the temporal dimension. This is where the time element comes in, for this temporal wandering in the tonal space directly corresponds to the confusion expressed in the lyric "I didn't know what time it was"—that is, this is high-level, artistic word painting of an uncommonly large scale. More specifically, each two-bar phrase closes on a consonant harmony, but that harmony is not the tonic, G major harmony. Thus, the music-textual confusion projects through time and through tonal space up to the last line of the first part of the Refrain: "And I'll say it was grand." With the first word of the first line of the Bridge, "Grand," in "Grand to be alive," we hear the first tonic G major harmony of the song. But although this chord is a tonic harmony, it is not a tonic harmony in the position of closure and key definition, which is (as stated earlier) at the *end* of a phrase. Indeed, in "I Didn't Know What Time It Was" the tonic harmony in its key-defining role occurs only at the end of the very last line of the lyrics, on "now!" in "I know what time it is now!"

While the Refrain delays the appearance of the key-defining tonic harmony in this remarkable way, the Verse does something similar, but in a much more straightforward manner. As shown by the chord symbol G6 above the staff in Ex. 3-54, the Verse begins with the tonic G chord modified by the added sixth.[45] In fact, each two-bar phrase begins with that chord. But the placement of the pure tonic chord in the key-defining end position does not occur until the final bar of the Verse, on the syllable "-ive." Nevertheless, the four occurrences of the tonic

Ex. 3-55. *"I Didn't Know What Time It Was": Melodic contour*

chord at the beginnings of the two-bar phrases clearly suggest that G major will be the key that delimits the *tonal space* of the song.

As can be seen in Ex. 3-55, melodic contour plays a significant role in shaping the expressive quality of "I Didn't Know What Time It Was." Attentive listening will show that the melody moves through tonal space in the descending direction over the first eight-bar period, accelerating over "lovely time it was, How sublime it was," but leaping upward abruptly on "too!" at the end of the period in bar 8.

In Ex. 3-55 the notes designated by asterisks carry the long-range descending line: B-A-G/B-A-G-F♯-E-D, with little excursions ("didn't know") and stepwise decorations ("time it was") attached to those notes. This long line would have completed its descent on the lower C (middle C) on the word "two" (note the asterisk enclosed in parentheses) were it not for the unexpected ascending leap to the upper C.

This dramatic upward leap prepares for the repetition of the first period that begins at bar 9 and makes the long descending trek over the melody of the second eight-bar period (Ex. 3-56). At the end of this period, in bar 15, the melody again

Ex. 3-56. *"I Didn't Know What Time It Was": Octave leap*

leaps abruptly and ecstatically upward, not to C as in bar 8, but to the high D on "grand," a full step higher than the C that set "too!" in bar 8. Yet, as striking as it is, this high D is not the apex of the melody.

The rhapsodic music of the Bridge then begins at bar 17 with the lyric

"Grand," repeated from the end of the previous bar. This particularly salient moment in the song coincides with the appearance of the first G major tonic harmony in the Refrain (see Ex. 3-53). Up to this point the peregrinations of the harmony have failed to locate the tonic home of the music. The beginning of the Bridge is further highlighted because the high E that sets "Grand" is the apex melodic note of the song (Ex. 3-57). In the first four-bar phrase of the Bridge, as in

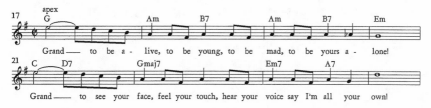

Ex. 3-57. *"I Didn't Know What Time It Was": Bridge*

the first two periods of the Refrain, the prevailing melodic direction is descending, and the same applies to the melody of the Bridge's second four-bar phrase, which imitates the ending of the first part of the Refrain by abruptly leaping upward to D on "own!" in bar 24. Some listeners will hear a long-range connection between the E of bar 17 ("Grand") and this D, since they are only a step apart.

Beginning in bar 29 of Chorus 2 (Ex. 3-58) we hear what we assume to be the final four-bar phrase of the song, a repetition of the melody of bars 13 through

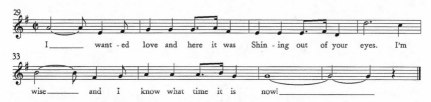

Ex. 3-58. *"I Didn't Know What Time It Was": Closing music*

16, but with new lyrics ("I wanted love . . ."). Now the histrionic ascending leap at the end of the phrase (again traversing the octave from D to D) sets "your eyes," confirming the love relation that underlies the lyrics of this song. However, as we might have suspected, this is not the end of the song. Instead, the appended four-bar phrase articulates the sanguine philosophical reflection that concludes the song: "I'm wise and I know what time it is now!"

What is truly remarkable about this final phrase, however, is its melody, which is identical to the melody of the first phrase of the Refrain, but is reharmonized by Rodgers so that instead of communicating the indeterminacy or "wandering" feeling of that phrase, it lies clearly within tonic harmony boundaries, expressing an affirmative and conclusive feeling that betokens a special and sophisticated artistry on the part of songwriter and lyricist.

■

DUKE ELLINGTON AND BILLY STRAYHORN, "SOMETHING TO LIVE FOR"
Lyrics by Billy Strayhorn and Duke Ellington
CD Track 15

Ex. 3-59. "Something to Live For": Leadsheet

LYRICS
Verse

1 I have almost ev'rything
2 A human could desire,
3 Cars and houses, bearskin rugs
4 To lie before my fire.
5 But there's something missing,
6 Something isn't there,
7 It seems I'm never kissing
8 The one whom I could care for.

Refrain
Chorus I
A

1 I want something to live for,
2 Someone to make my life
3 An adventurous dream.

A'

4 Oh, what wouldn't I give for
5 Someone who'd take my life
6 And make it seem gay

B (Bridge)

7 As they say it ought to be.
8 Why can't I have
9 Love like that brought to me?

Chorus 2
A'

10 My eye is watching the noon crowds
11 Searching the promenades
12 Seeking a clue

C

13 To the one who will someday
14 Be my something to live for.

The song dates from 1939, an extraordinary year in world affairs, as I indicated at the beginning of the discussion of the Rodgers and Hart song, "I Didn't Know What Time It Was," which dates from the same year. Compared with other songs from this year, which was also extraordinary with respect to the number of remarkable popular songs it produced, "Something to Live For" is not well known. There are several reasons for this, the song's unusual features and its technical difficulties being among them. In addition, "Something to Live For" was not a musical theater song, a movie song, but a big band item, associated with the Duke Ellington orchestra, for which Billy Strayhorn arranged a number of important works. "Something to Live For" did not, however, become a staple item in the Ellington orchestra's library, perhaps because of certain of the song's recondite characteristics. It was, to use a well-worn phrase, ahead of its time. Nor was its composer, Billy Strayhorn, known to the public. He was a professional musician's musician, especially highly regarded by black jazz and big band musicians, who knew him as a gifted pianist, arranger, and colleague of Duke Ellington. In assessing "Something to Live For" as a special song, it behooves us to bear in mind that Strayhorn (1915–1967) was 24 years old when he composed this music, perhaps with some collaborative effort on the part of Duke Ellington—an issue to which I shall return briefly below. First, however, let us give attention to the lyrics of "Something to Live For."

Lyrics

The lyrics of the Verse are set mainly in notes of equal duration (Ex. 3-59), which creates the kind of sing-song rhythm that is so characteristic of many verses and that is intended to imitate sung speech. As a result, we hear the lyrics as an unrelenting series of front-accented trochaic feet: "*I* have *al*most *ev*'ry thing." This is especially effective in the recitation of the list of philistinian possessions: "*Cars* and *hou*ses, *bear*skin rugs . . . ," with "bearskin rugs" evoking (at that time at least) the image of a sparsely clad maiden reclining bottom-up on the rug and gazing into the fireplace while her lover is seated alongside in a large chair, sipping a dry martini.

The second eight bars of the verse continue the end-rhyming design of the first eight, rhyming "missing" and "kissing," and "there" and "care." "Care," however, is followed by "for," which would spoil the rhyme were it not for its special role as the final word in the title phrase. In this strategic position at the end of the Verse it prepares the first statement of that title phrase, which follows immediately in bars 2 and 3 of the Refrain.

Change in melodic contour distinguishes the two halves of the sixteen-bar Verse and corresponds to the contrasting ideas of the lyrics. Predominantly descending gestures characterize the first eight bars, and the low notes at the bottom of each descending contour look ahead to a striking motion in the Refrain, namely, to the setting of "make my life" in bar 5 (see Ex. 3-59). Harmony also intensifies the ruefully reflective mood of the opening eight bars: the first of each two-bar pair presents a major harmony, the second a minor harmony—a "mood oscillation," as it were, establishing a contrast between a presumably contented and discontented atmosphere.

In the beginning of the second half of the Verse (bars 8 through 16) the ascending contours correspond to the new idea of the lyrics, to the effect that something is missing from the singer's life. We are soon told that this missing item is a love object.

The lyrics of the Refrain then elaborate on the attributes of this missing individual and on what he or she (the song is unisex) would bring to the persona represented by the singer. Clearly, the imaginary being has his or her work cut out for him or her. The expectations include a complete remake of the persona's life, and, furthermore, the attendant love relation is to be "brought" to the singer. However, lest we rush to the conclusion that the expectant lover plays a merely passive role, we are informed that he or she regularly keeps an eye peeled for just the right person, paying special attention to the noon crowds (in midtown Manhattan, presumably), which is quite a job in itself. All these expectations and desires are expressed in free or blank verse, in contrast to the rigid rhymed verse of the Verse.

Except for the very artistic remote rhymes, "dream" in bar 7 and "seem" in bar 15, which also connect in near-rhyme with "me" in bars 21–22, unification of the lyrics depends upon repetitions of key phrases: "take my life" matches "make my life"; "give for" matches "live for"; "brought to me" matches "ought to be." Strayhorn resists what must have been the temptation to rhyme "clue" near the end of the Refrain with "you," a word whose absence in these lyrics is excruciatingly apparent.

Verse

While the music of the first part of the Verse forms a very regular harmonic pattern that corresponds to its rhetorical function, the music of the second part (Ex. 3-60) is much freer and perambulatory, beginning in a key (Ab) that is remote from the main key and gradually moving back to it at the end of the Verse. In the context of these lyrics this kind of musical motion creates a feeling of brief disorientation, of "searching," which is a key word that occurs late in the lyrics of the Refrain. In projecting the idea of disorientation, perhaps connected with expectation, the ascending melodic contours of the second part of the Verse certainly

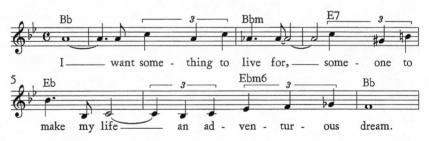

Ex. 3-60. "Something to Live For": Verse

play an important role (Ex. 3-60), conveying a basic atmosphere of uncertainty, soon to be resolved in the first part of the Refrain.

Refrain

Although the Refrain begins firmly in the tonic key, with the tonic harmony setting "I" in bar 1, the singer sings a special melodic note on this monosyllable, namely, the note located on the seventh step of the B♭ tonic scale (A)—a note that the syntax of tonal music normally requires to ascend to the tonic note, only a half step away on the eighth (tonic) note of that scale.[46] The resultant harmony is one of the most powerful and emotive in the vocabulary of classic American popular music. Perhaps the most familiar instance is the opening of Cole Porter's immortal and passionate love song, "Night and Day." Having said all this, I am now obliged to admit that "Something to Live For" does not behave according to textbook rules of tonal etiquette. First, the note on the seventh scale degree leaps up twice to the note above the tonic scale step, forming a short, oscillating pattern that emphasizes the text "want something to live for," almost like a verbal oscillation in the unsung voice (Ex. 3-61). When the melody returns from the second of the two upper notes it does not return to the original note (A), but to the note below it (A♭) that then sets "live for." What's more, the new note is supported by a minor harmony (B♭ minor), which creates a feeling of poignant

Ex. 3-61. "Something to Live For": Opening melody

intensity enhanced by the momentary uncertainty as to the subsequent course of the melody. This uneasiness resolves as the following phrase moves through "someone to" and ends the line on "make my life" over a major chord (E♭). It is here, on the lyrics "make my," that the melody leaps dramatically downward to the lowest notes in the song (B♭ and C), the first of these serving as nadir of the entire song. The entire eight-bar period (Ex. 3-61) then ends with "an adventurous dream," on the first long ascending contour in the Refrain, ending on the first pure tonic (B♭) harmony.

In general, Billy Strayhorn's melodies are characterized by the strategic placement of special notes, of which the A at the beginning of the Refrain is a striking example. Not only does he use special *diatonic* notes, but he also uses *chromatically altered* notes throughout the melody as a special way of enhancing the lyrics. A prime example is found at the beginning of bar 33 of the Refrain (Ex. 3-59), where F♯, altered (raised) diatonic scale degree 5, sets the first syllable of the poignant "someday."

Form

Because "Something to Live For" encompasses thirty-eight bars instead of the canonical thirty-two and contains other departures from the norms of this repertoire, a brief survey of its form seems useful. The reader may therefore wish to refer to the lead sheet of the entire song, provided by Ex. 3-59, while scanning the chart below.

Part	Bars	Subpart	Lyric	Length
A (Chorus 1)	1–8	a	"I"	8 bars
	9–14	a′	"Oh"	6 bars
B (Bridge)	15–18	b	"seem"	4 bars
	19–22	b′	"Why"	4 bars
A (Chorus 2)	23–28	a′	"Eye"	6 bars
C (Close)	29–38	c	"clue"	10 bars

Perhaps the two most unusual features of this design are the truncations designated *a′* and the relatively long final section, C, which introduces new melodic figures while retaining rhythmic features of the earlier music. The first truncation of subpart *a* (bars 9–14), in particular, lends a certain urgency to the lyrics by moving so quickly to the Bridge after only six bars of repetition. Similarly, the second truncation of subpart *a* (bars 23–28) leads suddenly to the closing section C, at which point the music begins to slow perceptibly while the lyrics project the idea of future happiness, which would seem to be a long way off.

As indicated in the chart, subpart *a′*, the music that follows the first eight-

Ex. 3-62. "Something to Live For": Bars 2–14

bar period of the Refrain (Ex. 3-62), begins by repeating the music of the first five bars, but of course with new lyrics, namely, those of lines 4 and 5 ("Oh, what wouldn't I give for/Someone who'd take my life"). Here the replication stops. From the low note that sets "life" (C) the melody soars upward ("and make it seem") to reach the high note on "seem" that is almost the apex of the melody (D).

Rhythmically, the long duration of this near-apex note on "seem" clearly associates it with the remote rhyming word "dream" back at bar 7. Here at the beginning of the Bridge (Ex. 3-63), when the melody arrives on the high note of

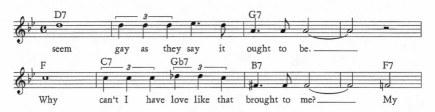

Ex. 3-63. "Something to Live For": Bridge

"seem" it stays there, intoning the lyrics "seem gay as they say it," with a strong inflection on "say" by moving up a step (to Eb). This has the effect of emphasizing the inner rhyme-pair "gay" and "say."

It is perhaps not coincidental that the note A, which sets that final lyric of the Bridge's first phrase, "ought to be," is the headnote of the melody of the Refrain of "Something to Live For," the first sung note in the Refrain. Moreover, the note that begins the next phrase, C in bar 19 ("Why"), is the second note in the melody that begins the Refrain. Thus, at this point in the song, midway through the Bridge, the music refers back to the very beginning, a beautiful and subtle joining of musical and textual ideas.

Ex. 3-64. "Something to Live For": Closing music

The closing phrase of the Bridge, which begins in bar 19 on line 8 of the lyrics ("Why can't I have love like that brought to me?"), is set harmonically in such a way that "brought to me" is supported by a harmony (B7) that is strategically located with respect to the tonic harmony that will begin Chorus II in bar 23.[47] The implications of this proximity are then fulfilled on the upbeat to the return of the main theme of the song, "My eye," in bars 22–23, and the last double period of the song begins with a partial repetition of the opening music.

The striking departure of the closing section from the preceding music becomes most evident when the voice suddenly ascends to sing "one" on the long near-apex pitch (D), recalling the special role of that note as discussed above in connection with its appearance at bar 15 on "seem." In terms of the lyrics, the near-rhyming association of "one" with "someday" and especially with the key word in the title, "something," is certainly noticeable.

As always, the final phrase of the song, line 14 of the lyrics, is informative in the semantic domain (Ex. 3-64). In the purely melodic sense, this proves to be unique, for its contour consists of the only other completely stepwise ascending line in the song, the other being line 5, "But there's something missing," back in bars 9–10. Thus, line 14 ("something to live for") can be considered as the answer, musically and semantically, to line 5. The final note of the melody (C) is the same as the second note of the melody in bar 2 of the Refrain, and is therefore heard as a clear reference to the opening music. But since the positions of the two opening, oscillating notes of the melody (A and C) are now reversed, the semantic twist seems to be of a positive nature: the upper note of the pair is now stabilized, perhaps suggesting if not a happy ending, at least a hopeful one![48]

Authorship

In an earlier paragraph I attributed the lyrics to Strayhorn, since, on the basis of the subtle and freely artistic treatment of the lyrics of the Refrain alone, which closely resembles that of his masterful "Lush Life," he was indubitably the one who wrote them. In any event, lyrics were not Duke Ellington's forte, if I may use that expression. Strayhorn and Ellington enjoyed a close professional relationship, beginning in 1938, when Ellington hired Strayhorn to work as an arranger-composer.[49] Gunther Schuller calls him "Duke's alter-ego of later years."[50] For our purposes, their association is perhaps less important than the recognition of the influence of the late-1930s big band ("swing") arrangements with their unusual harmonic changes on that repertoire and the resulting *enrichment* of the harmonic vocabulary of the American popular song, exemplified by "Something to Live For."[51]

CHAPTER FOUR

Songs from the Forties

■

HAROLD ARLEN, "THAT OLD BLACK MAGIC"
Lyrics by Johnny Mercer
CD Track 16 (with "There Will Never Be Another You")

LYRICS
A (1–32)

That old black magic has me in its spell.
That old black magic that you weave so well.
Those icy fingers up and down my spine.
The same old witchcraft when your eyes meet mine.
The same old tingle that I feel inside.
And then the elevator starts its ride.
And down and down I go, 'round and 'round I go
Like a leaf that's caught in the tide.

B (Bridge) (33–48)

I should stay away but what can I do
I hear your name and I'm aflame,
Aflame with such a burning desire
That only your kiss can put out the fire.

A' (49–64)

For you're the lover I have waited for.
The mate that fate had me created for
And ev'ry time your lips meet mine
Darling down and down I go,
'Round and 'round I go,

Coda (65–72)

In a spin,
Loving the spin I'm in,
Under that old black magic called love!

Ex. 4-1. "That Old Black Magic": Leadsheet

"That Old Black Magic" was written in 1942, which was, coincidentally, the first full year of U.S. participation in World War II. As a minor event in that dramatic historical context, Harold Arlen's song turned out to be the hit of Paramount Pictures' musical extravaganza, *Star Spangled Rhythm*, providing an early example of Hollywood's contribution to the war effort in the morale-boosting department, which simultaneously boosted the bank accounts of the movie people of course. *Star Spangled Rhythm* included appearances by many of the big stars of Hollywood: Bing Crosby, Bob Hope, Mary Martin, and Paulette Goddard.

Despite the romantic aura it projects, "That Old Black Magic" is not presented in the movie as a love aria, but rather it accompanies a song and dance number that features the remarkable performer Vera Zorina, lightly clad for maximum magical effect.[1]

Although its popularity was immediately evident, "That Old Black Magic" did not appear on "Your Hit Parade" until February 27, 1943, where it showed up in tenth place after having been recorded by the Glenn Miller Orchestra with Skip Nelson and the Modernaires, a popular singing group.[2] Subsequently it appeared on the show fifteen times, never rising to first, but attaining second place four times. Despite the presence of the many Hollywood personalities, *Star Spangled Rhythm* did not compete well with the many excellent movies of 1942, such as *Mrs. Miniver* (Greer Garson and Walter Pidgeon), *Casablanca* (Humphrey Bogart and Ingrid Bergman), and *Yankee Doodle Dandy* (James Cagney).[3]

Lyrics

According to Edward Jablonski, Harold Arlen credits Johnny Mercer's lyrics with the huge success of the song: "The words sustain your interest, make sense, contain memorable phrases, and tell a story. Without the lyric the song would be just another long song."[4]

These passionate lyrics, reminiscent of those Cole Porter wrote for "Night and Day" (1932), are among Mercer's best. The craft and inspiration are there; nothing seems forced. The poetic devices flow with the music and even seem often to drive it. The key phrase "black magic" inspires the elevator and tide metaphors and the more immediate physical responses expressed by "icy fingers," "aflame," and "burning," while the unforgettable images of motion, "down and down" and " 'round and 'round" perfectly match the melodic contours with which they are associated. Remarkably, Mercer delays the supercharged but cliché "love" until the very end, where it is equated with the titular "black magic." Mercer's deferential comment about the melody notwithstanding, in writing these wonderful lyrics, as will be shown, Mercer was very sensitive to the musical gestures of the melody and to the possibilities for word painting that they suggest.

The unisex lyrics have enabled the song to be rendered by many famous singers. Margaret Whiting recorded it in 1942, perhaps the earliest recording, and again in 1990, 48 years later. It is a timeless song.

Form and Melodic Design

Within the repertoire of American popular song, "That Old Black Magic" is very long, designed as it was for a specific scene in *Star Spangled Rhythm*. To render the component parts more visible, I indicate them on the displayed lyrics by the usual letters and include their corresponding bar numbers in parentheses. The A section alone consumes the traditional 32 bars.

With respect to contour, the melody of "That Old Black Magic" is remarkably diversified. In the first sixteen bars, which comprise two eight-bar *phrases* (not periods), much of the melodic action consists of a succession of repeated notes: G is repeated in the first eight measures and F in the second, preceded by the low B♭ ("That old"), which is the nadir pitch of the song (see Ex. 4-1). The inescapable suggestion of incantation that these repeated notes project jibes perfectly with Mercer's magical lyrics. Repetition has its limits, however, and Arlen composes the ends of these phrases in such a way as to break the repeated note succession while avoiding stereotyped repetition of the ending gestures themselves. This is shown in Ex. 4-2.

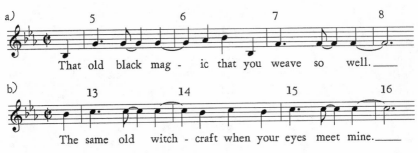

Ex. 4-2. "That Old Black Magic": Phrase endings

Ex. 4-2a displays the ending of the first eight-bar phrase on F ("weave so well"), which prepares the next succession of repeated notes that begins in bar 9 on that same note (F). Ex. 4-2b displays the quite different ending of the second eight-bar phrase, which involves the oscillation of only two notes, B♭ and C.

A remarkable change then begins at bar 17 ("The same old tingle"). Although this passage still emphasizes the repeated notes (G), the motion up to blue note D♭, the first chromatic note in the song, which sets "I," signals a change, especially since that note is the highest yet (Ex. 4-3).

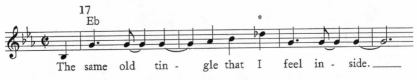

Ex. 4-3. "That Old Black Magic": Special note

It is precisely in the following passage that the elevator metaphor develops, and the initial plunge of that device departs from the high E♭ that sets "-tor." This note succeeds the previous D♭ as the highest note in the melody. The "plunge" from E♭ lands on F ("starts its ride"), and it is here that the unexpected occurs: a change of harmony (*down* to D♭) that momentarily takes the music out of the home key of E♭. Ex. 4-4 summarizes the notation of this startling kinesthetic effect. In the final phrase of the A section that follows the music shown in Ex. 4-4, the lyrics "And down and down I go, 'round and 'round I go" set the succession of two literally descending two-bar phrases, shown in Ex. 4-5. With its ending on

Ex. 4-4. "That Old Black Magic": Downward leap

Ex. 4-5. "That Old Black Magic": Text painting

middle C, this pictorial gesture almost, but not quite, reaches the nadir pitch of the song, the low B♭.

Dramatic descending leaps followed by compensatory ascending contours characterize the melody of the Bridge. Each of the two eight-bar phrases begins with the same pattern, the second a downward transposition of the first by three half steps. Ex. 4-6 displays these patterns. I draw particular attention to the "8ve

Ex. 4-6. "That Old Black Magic": Bridge

Ex. 4-7. *"That Old Black Magic": Octave leap*

leap" marked on both a) and b) in Ex. 4-6. This, the largest leap in the entire song, has special expressive impact here, but perhaps even more when it occurs for the third and last time in the final section of the song, as shown in Ex. 4-7, setting the sensuous lyric, "lips meet."

I previously mentioned the fleeting appearance of the blue note Db (see Ex. 4-3). In the final section of the song (A′) this melodic note comes into its own, setting the memorable line "The mate that fate had me created for" with its triple rhyme, "mate," "fate," "create." In terms of the form of the song, it is exactly here that the A′ section begins to differ from section A (Ex. 4-8).

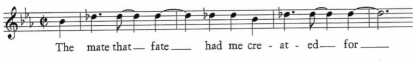

Ex. 4-8. *"That Old Black Magic": Special note*

In the artistic ending of "That Old Black Magic" the "down and down I go, 'round and 'round I go" music returns. As at the end of section A, this leads the melody to the tonic note Eb. Now, however, that note of closure is extended through yet another eight bars to form a final magical incantation in which the lyric "spin" plays a key role, preserving the images of motion the lyricist has created.

Rhythm

In Arlen's sheet music arrangement of "That Old Black Magic," the pianist's left hand plays the figure shown in Ex. 4-9 for some thirty-one bars, that is, throughout section A.[5] This perpetual motion rhythm, aptly called an *ostinato*, which is a feature of "That Old Black Magic," is reminiscent of Ravel's *Bolero*, Cole Porter's "When They Begin the Beguine," and much exotic dance music. It reflects the influence of Latin American music, which, in 1942, was well entrenched in American popular song, having made inroads at several important junctures,

Ex. 4-9. *"That Old Black Magic"*:
Ostinato

going back at least to the 1920s, with its popularity reaching the status of a craze on many occasions.

The obsessive rhythmic figure of the melody of "That Old Black Magic" is notated as dotted quarter-eighth tied to quarter-quarter, which divides the eight regular pulses (eighth notes) of the bar into three groups, as shown in Ex. 4-9. More specifically, the melody groups the eight pulses of the left-hand ostinato into 3 + 3 + 2, the ubiquitous Latin rhythm, which will be familiar to those with knowledge of the rhumba, samba, and other Latin American dance forms.

■

HARRY WARREN, "THERE WILL NEVER BE ANOTHER YOU"
Lyrics by Mack Gordon
CD Track 16 (with "That Old Black Magic")

LYRICS
Verse

This is our last dance together,
Tonight soon will be long ago,
And in our moment of parting,
This is all I want you to know:

Refrain
Chorus I
A (double period)

There will be many other nights like this,
And I'll be standing here with someone new,
There will be other songs to sing,
Another fall, another spring,
But there will never be another you.

Ex. 4-10. "There Will Never Be Another You": Leadsheet

A' (double period)

There will be other lips that I may kiss,
But they won't thrill me like yours used to do,
Yes, I may dream a million dreams,
But how can they come true,
If there will never ever be another you?

Like virtually all of Harry Warren's songs, "There Will Never Be Another You" was written for a motion picture, in this case for *Iceland* (1942), a forgettable movie that featured ice skating star Sonja Henie. In the movie, Joan Merrill renders the song twice in a nightclub scene, once in ballad style, once in a torchy arrangement, backed by a band. The song is only loosely connected with the plot of the movie, such as it is.

Although as a songwriter Warren got his start on Broadway, his mature career unfolded in Hollywood, where he worked for no fewer than four of the major studios: Warner Brothers, 20th Century Fox, Metro Goldwyn Mayer, and Paramount Pictures.

Born in Brooklyn in 1893, Harry Warren was given the name Salvadore Guaragna by his immigrant Italian parents. Like several other prominent songwriters of his era he exchanged his name for one that was more accessible to the public and one that did not elicit ethnic biases and pigeonholing.

It seems that because Warren was connected with Hollywood and not with Broadway for the major portion of his career, his name often does not appear with those of his contemporaries among the major songwriters of the period.[6] Ironically, and because of their movie origins, his songs probably reached a much larger and more diversified public than did those that came out of traditional musical theater.

Among the very popular songs from Warren's pen are: "I Only Have Eyes For You" (1934); "September In The Rain" (1937); "Jeepers Creepers" (1938); "At Last" (1942); "Serenade in Blue" (1942); "You'll Never Know" (1943); "On The Atcheson, Topeka And The Santa Fe" (1945). Of these, "September In The Rain," "Jeepers Creepers," and "You'll Never Know" attained first place on "Your Hit Parade," with "You'll Never Know" occupying that position nine times.[7]

In a curious turnabout, the 1932 movie musical *42nd Street* (with Ruby Keeler, Dick Powell, and Ginger Rogers) was revised and staged as a Broadway musical in the 1980–81 seasons, winning a Tony award. Unfortunately, Harry Warren died in 1981, so he was unable to enjoy this career-spanning tribute to the fullest.

Form and Lyrics

Mack Gordon, who wrote the lyrics for "There Will Never Be Another You," collaborated with a number of songwriters during his professional life. With Harry Warren he created the words (and titles) for "Chattanooga Choo Choo," "You'll Never Know," and other well-known songs. Although not in the same class as, say, Johnny Mercer or Lorenz Hart, Gordon is regarded as a talented and musically sensitive lyricist. These qualities are evident here.

In the lyrics of the Verse of "There Will Never Be Another You," the singer sets the scene: the lovers are about to separate, and he or she wishes to impart a final message. The Refrain touches upon the complex emotional state, in which the singer foresees future love relationships as inevitable but never as satisfying as the one about to be dissolved. This is expressed in the title phrase, which is delayed until the end of the B section, bars 13–16: "But there will never be another you." Just how complex this situation can become is suggested by the final line of the lyrics, couched in the interrogatory mode: "If there will never ever be another you?" Possibly the singer holds out some small hope that there might be "another you," juxtaposing "never" and "ever" for emphasis, and creating yet another feature that associates this song with the torch-song genre.[8]

"There Will Never Be Another You" is a four-part song, forming the pattern ABAB′, where each part spans eight bars. However, while the A sections correspond to two lines of lyrics, the B sections correspond to three lines. The musical effect of this is one of intensification or compression in the B sections: instead of the two ideas expressed in the A sections, the B sections contain three ideas. Gordon has matched Warren's melodic patterns in a sensitive and musical way.

> A (1–8):
> There will be many other nights like this,
> And I'll be standing here with someone new,
> B (9–16):
> There will be other songs to sing,
> Another fall, another spring,
> But there will never be another you.
> A (17–24):
> There will be other lips that I may kiss,
> But they won't thrill me like yours used to do,
> B′(25–32):
> Yes, I may dream a million dreams,
> But how can they come true,
> If there will never ever be another you?

The rhyme scheme of the Refrain works against the highly patterned form of the melody in the ingenious way summarized in the succession shown below, where the A sections present the same *ab* pair, while the B and B′ sections vary. Notice, however, that the three lines of B′ reverse the pattern of B, with the two rhyming lines preceding the unrhymed line in B and the reverse occurring in B′.

> A: *ab*   (this/new)
> B: *ccb*   (sing/spring/you)
> A: *ab*   (kiss/do)
> B′: *ebb* (dreams/true/you)

And as a very nice touch, Gordon leaves one line, line *e* ("dreams"), unrhymed, which lends it a special semantic emphasis that is perfectly in accord with the idea of the lyrics. Thus, the somewhat irregular rhyme scheme offers a marked contrast to the regular rhythms of the melody of "There Will Never Be Another You."

Melody and Harmony

Perhaps most immediately apparent about the melody of "There Will Never Be Another You" are the long strings of notes of the same value that characterize this song. Consider the first four-bar phrase (Ex. 4-11), in which the first seven syl-

Ex. 4-11. *"There Will Never Be Another You": Opening phrase*

lables are set by notes of the same value: quarter notes. In addition, the contour formed by these notes is unidirectional; after the seventh note ("-er"), there is an abrupt leap downward to a longer note on "nights," followed by the short note on "like" (eighth note). The four-bar phrase then ends on a very long duration: the whole note tied to the dotted half note. Thus, the melody features notes of the same duration within a unidirectional contour, a hallmark of this beautiful song. In addition, stepwise motion predominates; there are only two leaps, to and from the syllable "er." On the other hand, the close of the phrase has a distinctive pattern, the long-short dotted quarter–eighth followed by the very long duration on "this," which highlights the evocative lyric, "nights like this."

The second four-bar phrase of the Refrain of "There Will Never Be Another You" strongly resembles the first with respect to its ascending trajectory (Ex. 4-12). This melodic line, however, is higher altogether than that of the first phrase, ascending, in fact, to touch the apex note of the song (E♭) on "with."

These two phrases (Examples 4-11 and 4-12), which consist of long strings of notes of the same duration, are hardly experienced as monotonous, for by pro-

Ex. 4-12. *"There Will Never Be Another You": Second phrase*

jecting successively higher contours they heighten the emotional message of the lyrics. Moreover, the rhythmic changes that break the long patterns correspond to a strategic placement of key harmonic changes. These changes are very audible at the ends of each phrase and can be seen in the notation of Ex. 4-10 at bars 2–3, which matches "nights like this" with bars 6–7 ("someone new").

In the traditional "barform" pattern *aab*, the first two four-bar phrases (*aa*) of the Refrain culminate in the eight-bar phrase (*b*), shown in Ex. 4-13. This phrase

Ex. 4-13. *"There Will Never Be Another You": Bars 2–16*

encompasses not four bars but eight, unfolding a very long string of quarter notes. This feature, however, is secondary to two others. First, the melody begins with a strong statement of the apex note E♭, emphatically setting "will." Second, in a marked contrast to the ascending contours of the first two phrases, we now hear a succession of three descending contours, corresponding to the three lines of the lyrics projected in this B section.[9] Each contour ends with an oscillating figure in which a lower note decorates a note directly above it. In bar 14, on "be another you," this figure multiplies itself and is heard twice in succession, a beautiful melodic detail.

In the final phrase of the song, which begins in bar 29 (Ex. 4-14), we hear the final descending melodic contour. At its beginning this phrase resembles phrase 3 (Ex. 4-13), especially the upward leap on "there will." The goal of the phrase, however, is quite different: it moves relentlessly to the tonic note E♭ in the final bar, with the poignant interrogatory lyrics "If there will never ever be

Ex. 4-14. *"There Will Never Be Another You": Final phrase*

another you?" In addition to the stepwise motion so characteristic of this song, this final phrase includes two prominent leaps. The first of these (x), on "there will," matches the second (x') on "ever," since both involve the notes B♭ and E♭. The reader will recall that E♭ is the special apex note. Here it occurs in its apex register (x) and an octave lower (x'a) as well. As a final and very sensitive melodic detail, the setting of "-oth-er" in the next-to-last bar may be heard as yet another form of the oscillating figure shown in Ex. 4-13.

Verse

The Verse of "There Will Never Be Another You," which consists of the standard sixteen bars, is very recitativelike (Ex. 4-1). Its motivic relation to the Refrain may at first seem elusive, but there are connections. For example, it begins with the first two notes of the Refrain, but placed an octave higher. In fact, throughout the Verse an emphasis is placed upon the note B♭, which is the headnote of the Refrain and is otherwise prominent there.

We also hear the oscillating figure of the Refrain (Ex. 4-13) upside down as well as in its regular descending configuration. And a particular two-note melodic fragment that is of special importance to the lyrics of the Refrain occurs prominently twice: the setting of "last dance" by the notes D-C in bar 2 of the Verse and again at the beginning of "This is all" in bar 12. Finally, the melody at the end of the Verse ("all I want you to know") replicates exactly the ascending scale segment at the beginning of the Refrain. Thus, although the Verse does not include the kind of elaborate composing of connections with the Refrain that we might hear in a Gershwin song, it does relate effectively to the Refrain and prepares some of its characteristic melodic features.

■

COLE PORTER, "EV'RY TIME WE SAY GOODBYE"
Lyrics by Cole Porter
CD Track 17

LYRICS
Verse

1 We love each other so deeply
2 That I ask you this, sweetheart,
3 Why should we quarrel ever,
4 Why can't we be enough clever
5 Never to part?

Ex. 4-15. "Ev'ry Time We Say Goodbye": Leadsheet

Refrain

Chorus I

A (period)

1 Ev'ry time we say goodbye

2 I die a little,

3 Ev'ry time we say goodbye

4 I wonder why a little,

B (period)

5 Why the gods above me
6 Who must be in the know
7 Think so little of me
8 They allow you to go.

Chorus 2
A' (period)

9 When you're near there's such an air
10 Of spring about it,
11 I can hear a lark somewhere
12 Begin to sing about it.

B' (period)

13 There's no love song finer
14 But how strange the change
15 From major to minor
16 Ev'ry time we say goodbye,
17 Ev'ry single time we say goodbye.

On June 6, 1944, Allied troops landed on the coast of northern France, with the U.S. Expeditionary Force assigned to what was designated "Omaha Beach" in Normandy, the final resting place for many young Americans. This monumental event, which we know as D-Day, was no doubt the greatest historical occurrence of the year and perhaps of the century, for it signaled the end of World War II in Europe and the end of the Nazi regime in Germany. Only the dropping of the atomic bombs on Japan the following year, ending the war in the Pacific, was of greater significance.

At this point in history, it seems that every other event in 1944 was subsidiary to those connected with the war. Amazingly, however, cultural activities in the United States continued to flourish. The Hollywood movie people were especially prolific, producing *Double Indemnity* (Barbara Stanwyck), *Gaslight* (Ingrid Bergman, Charles Boyer), *Cover Girl* (Rita Hayworth, Gene Kelly), and the saccharine *Going My Way* (Bing Crosby, Barry Fitzgerald), which nevertheless won the Best Picture Award of the Motion Picture Academy. *On the Town*, by twenty-six-year-old Leonard Bernstein, appeared on Broadway, and two musicals by fifty-three-year-old Cole Porter opened, one at each end of the year:

Mexican Hayride on January 28, and *Seven Lively Arts* on December 7, perhaps unwittingly celebrating the third anniversary of the entry of the United States into World War II, by which time it was clear that the war would soon be over. Among the top performers of music chosen by *Downbeat* magazine was jazz pianist Mel Powell, later to teach composition at Yale (and a friend of the author).

In concert music, Aaron Copland composed *Appalachian Spring*, for which he won the 1945 Pulitzer Prize. Roger Sessions completed his *Second Symphony*, as did Samuel Barber. Among the prominent American figures in painting were Milton Avery, Clyfford Still, Lyonel Feininger, Mark Tobey, and Robert Mother-well, the latter an influential figure in the movement that became known as abstract expressionism. It was a fecund period in the arts, and American popular song continued to flourish, as did jazz, especially the new style, dubbed bebop, of which trumpet player Dizzy Gillespie and alto saxophonist Charlie Parker were the primary representatives.

The foundations of many significant features of present-day science and technology became visible in this year: the first computer was created at Harvard by Howard Aiken, DNA was isolated by Oswald Avery, William Doering synthesized quinine, and the United States Army developed a jet-propelled airplane.

Cole Porter composed "Ev'ry Time We Say Goodbye" for *Seven Lively Arts*, a grandiose review conceived by Broadway entrepreneur and sometime lyricist Billy Rose, which ran for a modest 183 performances. The culturally ambitious review included music for ballet by Stravinsky (*Scènes de Ballet*) and scenery designed by Salvador Dali. Benny Goodman, then a major figure on the popular music scene, had a part in the review and also conducted the pit band, which consisted of name players from his Quintet (for example, Teddy Wilson). It was the Goodman Quintet's recording, with vocalist Peggy Mann, that brought "Ev'ry Time We Say Goodbye" to "Your Hit Parade," where it appeared once and only once, in ninth place, on February 10, 1945.

Despite its rather unpromising nascence, "Ev'ry Time We Say Goodbye" became a standard work in the repertoire of Cole Porter songs, due both to the cleverness of the composer's lyrics and to the affective musical setting of the words, which, at the time of its release certainly touched many who had experienced sad farewells throughout the war.

In line 4 of the Verse, which is not on the compact disc, it is startling to hear the reversal of the normal syntax that yields "enough clever" instead of "clever enough." It is clearly apparent that Porter did this in order to provide the end rhyme for line 3's "ever" as well as to juxtapose the end word "clever" and the rhyming word "Never" at the beginning of the very next line, line 5, thus producing an inner rhyme as well as the rhyme chain "ever," "clever," and "never." As a bonus, the syllable "ev" carries forward to the first syllable of the first word in the title phrase, "Ev'ry," creating a sonic link between the Verse and the onset of the Refrain.

Indeed, the rhyme scheme of the Verse is subtle and innovative in other ways. For instance, although lines 1 and 5 have no end rhymes in the usual sense, "deeply" at the end of line 1 finds a near-rhyme in the first syllable of "sweetheart," and "part" at the end of Line 5 finds its rhyme in the second syllable of that same word. Thus, the processes of rhyming, near rhyming, inner rhyming, and remote rhyming forge sonic connections as well as semantic associations at a deeper level of meaning.

Rhyme and near rhyme are also everywhere in the Refrain, creating luminous threads that run through the lyrics. Thus, over the first four lines the key vowel sound is the "i" in "time" and "goodbye." "Die" in line 2 provides the first link, continuing through "why" in lines 4 and 5. In lines 6 through 8 the rhyming words are "know" and "go," the latter a remote alliteration with respect to "gods" in line 5. And in lines 1 through 8, which correspond to the first double period of music (bars 1 through 16), Porter makes ample use of exact repetition both of the title phrase and of words that rhyme words in the title phrase—in particular, "me," which rhymes "we." In these various ways he creates an intricate and interesting verbal fretwork that amplifies the idea of the song: the parting of lovers, with all of its emotional overtones.

In Chorus 2 of the Refrain, this elaborate interweaving of words by rhyme and near rhyme includes alliteration based upon the sibilant "s" sound ("spring," "somewhere," "sing," "song," "strange"), such that I am tempted to suggest—at the risk of exaggerating—that these derive from "say" in the title phrase. Be that as it may, it is the last of these "s" words, "strange," that initiates the oft-cited lines: "But how strange the change from major to minor." And, I should point out, it is the "i" vowel in "minor," that leads so beautifully to "goodbye" at the end of lines 17 and 18.

Remarkably, it is "the change from major to minor" that underlies key moments in the music, word-painting the idea of parting followed by reconciliation expressed verbally in the lyrics. The first instance of this is not in line 16 ("From major to minor"), as generally thought, but in the oscillation of harmonies that occurs three times at the very beginning of the song. Each of the first three bars of music begins on a major harmony (E♭) and is followed directly by a minor harmony (Cm).[10] Since the vocalist sings the title phrase on one note throughout the first three bars, the only motion results from the repeated change in harmony. Indeed, the repeated note (eight times!) at the very beginning of the melody is the hallmark of this song, one that has attracted the attention of critics.[11] Clearly this is an instance of word painting, representing the kind of sorrowful hesitation that is so characteristic of farewells.

Much later in the song, in bars 26–28 (lines 14–16), we hear the famous reference to "the change from major to minor." On the lyric "major to minor" in bar 28, the harmony changes from A♭ to A♭m to give the effect of the change to minor to which the lyrics refer.[12]

The "change from major to minor" occurs at other strategic and hyper-expressive locations in the song. After the oscillation of the opening bars, the most striking of these is the minor sonority on "why" (bar 8) in "I wonder why" (line 4). In the corresponding location in Chorus 2, the word "sing" in "begin to sing about it" (line 12) is set by the major version of the minor sonority back in bar 8. Although the two locations are remote in time, the correspondence in location with respect to Chorus 1 and Chorus 2 renders the change, in this case from minor to major, absolutely lucid and intensely expressive.

Of course there is much more to the melodic design of "Ev'ry Time We Say Goodbye" than the prominent dualism of major and minor. Perhaps the most apparent feature of the large-scale melody is the gradual ascent that starts from the recitation on "Ev'ry time we say goodbye," continues at bar 5 with a repetition of the same line at a higher level, and again on a repeated note (B♭), and culminates on a still higher level at bar 9 with the exhortatory "Why the gods above me." Here the high note (E♭) is almost the apex, or "apex-1." Porter saves the true apex for later, where it sets a key word in the lyrics. From this high note the melody begins a slow descent, pausing on "know" in bar 12 at the end of the phrase, and continuing from "Think so little of me" to the end of the new phrase in bar 16, and the end of the first part of the song, a double eight-bar period.

Particularly poignant is the change from the major harmony that sets "know" in bar 12 to the minor harmony that sets "Think" in bar 13. Remarkably, the two chords are the same as those mentioned above that are involved in "the change from major to minor" further on in the song.

The lyrics of the second part of "Ev'ry Time We Say Goodbye" return to the more reflective mood of the beginning: "When you're near . . . ," and the melody repeats the music of the first part, ascending slowly to the high E♭ at bar 25, where the singer declaims "There's no love song finer." On "love" the melody reaches one step higher to the apex note of the entire song (F), thus emphasizing this special adjective, its only appearance in the song after its occurrence as a verb at the very beginning of the Verse ("We love each other . . ."). The slow descent of the melody then begins, just as in the first part of the song, but differs for the special lines "But how strange the change/From major to minor." This sentient interpolation then leads directly to the titular phrase, with no punctuation. That is, the change occurs "Ev'ry Time We Say Goodbye." Thus, the final lines reveal the deeper sentimental meaning of the change of mode. Further, although the second and final repetition of the title phrase begins on the same note as the first statement in bars 1–3, now the melody descends to the tonic note (E♭) on "goodbye," which creates a feeling of finality and perhaps a closing touch of irony, since the parting and reconciliation that underlie the song presumably continue—especially when the song is sung again!

As in all of Cole Porter's songs, rhythmic patterns are informed by the natural flow and accentuations of spoken language. We hear this in the opening of the Refrain in the long-short-longer setting of the three syllables of "Ev'ry time," which gives special emphasis to "time." The pattern then continues, emphasizing "-bye" in "goodbye," and the next long duration is on "die," bar 4. Thus, the long notes set the rhyming syllables "time," "bye," and "die" to form a sonic chain. In the second part of the song (from bar 17), as well as in the first part, the long notes connect three pairs of rhyming words between lines: "near-hear," "air-where," and "Spring-sing." Indeed, the "threeness" that the key words "ev'ry time" establish at the very beginning of the song pervades its rhythmic patterns, and there are many instances—for example, in the fast succession that sets "a little" in bar 4.

As for harmony, here we have a song written in 1944, well past the peak of the big bands, yet there is no evidence of the influence (infusion) of richer harmonies from jazz and the big swing band arrangements. On the other hand, the *harmonic progressions* are innovative, and in contemporary interpretations they lend themselves to a variety of "enrichment" (enhancement) techniques— indeed, they invite the application of these procedures by musicians steeped in the idioms of modern jazz and arranging.

■

HOAGY CARMICHAEL, "HOW LITTLE WE KNOW"
Lyrics by Johnny Mercer
CD Track 18

LYRICS
Chorus I

1 Maybe it happens this way,
2 Maybe we really belong together,
3 But after all,
4 How little we know.
5 Maybe it's just for a day,
6 Love is as changeable as the weather
7 And after all,
8 How little we know.

Ex. 4-16. "How Little We Know": Leadsheet

Bridge

9 Who knows why an April breeze never remains?
10 Why stars in the trees hide when it rains?
11 Love comes along casting a spell,
12 Will it sing you a song, will it say a farewell?
13 Who can tell?

Chorus 2

14 Maybe you're meant to be mine;
15 Maybe I'm only supposed to stay
16 In your arms awhile,
17 As others have done.
18 Is this what I've waited for?
19 Am I the one?
20 Oh, I hope in my heart that it's so
21 In spite of how little we know.

In the movie from which it comes (*To Have and Have Not*), the song is rendered by twenty-year-old Lauren Bacall, draped invitingly over the barroom piano to reveal some of her outstanding features, Hoagy seated at the piano, in bow tie, with elastic bands holding up his shirt-sleeves and a cigarette dangling from the side of his mouth, while a small bourbon languishes at the end of the music rack.[13]

But for virtually all of the popular songs in this repertoire, time and usage have erased associations with their origin, and they remain context-free. In the case of "How Little We Know," many listeners will be unaware of the movie's circumstances and simply experience a beautifully poignant exploration of feelings about a love relationship.

Although the movie was (and is) very popular, primarily because of Humphrey Bogart's presence in the starring role, "How Little We Know" was never on "Your Hit Parade." In assaying this fact, however, we must bear in mind that placement on "Your Hit Parade," although always of interest as a measure of public response, never certified quality. For example, "The Hut Sut Song" first appeared on "Your Hit Parade" June 14, 1941, and stayed on for twelve weeks, attaining first place three times. I would guess that very few of the readers will know or recall that song, which posterity, in its merciful wisdom, has seen fit to discard.

Lyrics

The lyrics for "How Little We Know" were written by one of the best, Johnny Mercer, who was himself a singer, actor, and public figure. They read like a long prose-poem, long because of the cinematic requirement for music in the elaborate setting of a barroom on the exotic French island of Martinique, with the gorgeously exotic Lauren Bacall, in her debut role, emoting all over the piano as she sings Mercer's touching lines.

The lyricist has divided the lyrics of Chorus 1 into two four-line stanzas, unified by the process of "stanzaic rhyme," so that line 5 rhymes line 1, line 6 rhymes
line 2, and so on, forming the pattern *abcd/a'b'c'd'*, in which the last two lines
of each stanza rhyme by simple replication. As a result, both line 4 and line 8
carry the titular phrase "How Little We Know."

Even with the regular rhyme scheme of the first two stanzas, the verses have
a colloquial quality, perhaps because of the perennial expressions "after all" and
"really." At any event, Mercer has created very appealing and apposite contexts
for the two appearances of the cliché title phrase "How Little We Know," which
does not occur again until the very last line of the lyrics.

A marked change of character comes with the lyrics of the Bridge, which
feature four interrogative lines, beginning with the alliterations "Who," "Why,"
and "Will," and ending with "Who." Here "Love" comes into the picture for the
second time (after line 6), metaphorically personified to cast a spell, to sing, and,
sadly, possibly to say farewell. The pathos implied in the eventuality of the departure of love is then intensified, with a strong tinge of irony, in the final and
special line 13: "Who can tell?" which is emphasized by the special Latinesque
rhythm short-short-long that closes the Bridge.

Unlike those of Chorus 1, the lyrics of Chorus 2 of "How Little We Know,"
beginning with line 14, do not exhibit a regular rhyme scheme. In fact, rhyming
seems to be in short supply, except for the final couplet, with its end rhymes "so"
and "know" and the rhymed pair "done" and "one." Indeed, the lyrics of Chorus 2
are considerably more prose-like, reflecting the uncertainty of the singer with
respect to the intentions of the loved one and even referring to his (or her) prior
history in line 17, "As others have done," which suggests a negative conclusion to
the love affair. The final rhymed couplet then comes in rather to suggest, strongly
but rather smugly, that although the outcome is unknown, chances are that the
persona represented by the singer is "the one."

These lyrics, which articulate the uncertainties of love, are very much in
the Cole Porter tradition. They also reflect the wartime uncertainties of personal
relations, to which many viewers of the movie would have been sensitive, and,
more immediately, they were very close to the tense situation portrayed in *To
Have and Have Not*, which involved large-scale wartime hostilities as well as the
smaller and no doubt more intriguing mock-hostile but amorous scenario unfolding between Humphrey and Lauren.

Rhythm

Rhythm is definitely in the foreground of "How Little We Know," especially
on first hearing. This is because of the syncopations that break up the succes-

sions of notes of the same duration. This occurs right away, in bar 1, where the first syllable of "happens" is stretched out for an extra pulse. It occurs again in bar 3, where the first syllable of "really" is given the same treatment. In addition, there are longer syncopations over the bar lines, but these are more conventional. Effectively the succession of short notes or, in rhythmic terms, pulses, divides each bar of music into eight units, two of which coalesce to form the syncopation. Now, eight-beat rhythms like this in American popular song have a common origin: the "Latin" rhythms transmitted to North America from Africa through South America and the Caribbean—Cuba, in particular, of which the best known are the rhumba and samba dance rhythms.[14]

Hoagy Carmichael's eight-beat rhythm in "How Little We Know" is very appropriate to the setting of the movie on the colorful French Caribbean island of Martinique. It also presents the Latin beat in a very subtle way, dividing the eight-pulse succession into the 3 + 3 + 2 grouping that corresponds to the pattern of the lyrics. This is shown schematically below for bar 1:

> 3   3   2
> May-be   it hap-pens   this way

Note that although "happens" contains only two syllables, the syncopation extends the first syllable, "hap," by one pulse, so that the entire word consumes three pulses. The reader can easily count and/or clap this eight-beat rhythmic pattern, placing the emphases (accents) as indicated by bold, thus:
1 2 3 **1** 2 3 **1** 2

Of course the Latin element is not always apparent in "How Little We Know." Still, whenever the short pulses are in operation, it is not very far away. For example, the astute reader will hear Latin rhythmic fragments in the Bridge, which begins in bar 16 (Ex. 4-16), each time the four-note figure from the opening music is sung, since each of these figures ends with a syncopation (expansion) that allows an eight-beat pattern to peek through, as it were. This repetitive succession breaks in the most striking way in bar 30 on the couplet "will it say a farewell? Who can tell?" At that point in the song a new rhythm comes in, beginning with six regular pulses in bar 30 and ending with the idiomatic Flamenco rhythm short-short-long on "Who can tell?" which Carmichael and Mercer surely intended to have a humorous effect.

Harmony

In Chorus 1 and Chorus 2, the harmony is relatively simple; the musical action focuses upon rhythm and lyrics. Indeed, for almost four bars the melody outlines a single chord, the tonic, with a single embellishing note (F). The titular phrase, "How Little We Know," and the music that comes just before it, changes the orientation of the harmony away from the tonic (to the dominant), not only fulfilling that hoary aesthetic requirement, variety, but also keeping the harmonic design open for the return to the tonic with the beginning of the second period (bar 9).

Earlier I mentioned the marked change in the character of lines 9–12 of the lyrics when they appear in the Bridge (Ex. 4-16, bars 17–32). Along with these more intricate and poetic lines comes a radical change in harmonic style from the stable motions of Chorus 1. After the first four bars of the Bridge ("Who knows why an April breeze never remains"), which stay in the tonic key of A♭, the song embarks upon a series of harmonic excursions, each spanning four bars and corresponding to one of the rhetorical queries in the lyrics. This is a beautiful instance of harmonic analogue: the harmonic excursions are themselves exploratory, leading not to a definitive goal but forward to the next question. Even without a knowledge of the mechanism of harmonic progression in tonal music, the listener intuits the semantics of this series of motions and interprets them in the poetically interrogative terms expressed by the lyrics.

Melody and Form

Finally, something more about the melodic design and the form of "How Little We Know" seems in order. Perhaps the most interesting part of the song from the standpoint of melody and form is Chorus 1, which consists of a double (not repeated) eight-bar period. As we can see in Ex. 4-17, the internal organization of the eight-bar period does not conform to the normal succession of four-bar phrases. Instead, there is an initial two-bar phrase, labelled A, that sets line 1 of the lyrics, followed by a three-bar phrase, labelled A′, which contains lines 2 and 3, then the title line "how little we know," which occupies three bars, including the long duration of the final word, "know." This last phrase is labeled

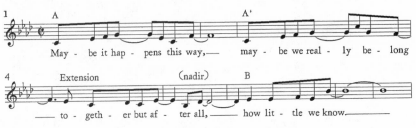

Ex. 4-17. "How Little We Know": Initial period

B in Ex. 4-17. Notice that the phrase labelled A′ begins like phrase A (hence the prime symbol attached to the second A), but then extends to accommodate line 3 of the lyrics. Thus, instead of the four bar + four bar paradigm the period consists of two bars + three bars + three bars. The musical effect of this remarkable asymmetrical arrangement resembles that of a rhythmic syncopation; indeed, it is exactly analogous to the reversal of a typical eight-beat "Latin" pattern: 2 + 3 + 3 reverses 3 + 3 + 2. However we might characterize this measure grouping, the feeling it generates certainly resembles "displacement" or the interruption of an expected normal continuation after phrase A. The two bars given to the final word of the title phrase "know" then serve to restore the balance of the eight-bar phrase, matching the two bars of phrase A and preparing for the repetition of the 2 + 3 + 3 measure grouping.

In contrast to the asymmetrical Chorus 1 and Chorus 2, the Bridge, which begins in bar 17, unfolds through a regular succession of four-bar phrases, four of them, to be precise, totaling sixteen bars. It is the sixteen bars of the Bridge (instead of the usual eight bars) that enlarge the total length of "How Little We Know" to forty-eight instead of the traditional thirty-two bars.

Like Chorus 1, Chorus 2 introduces unexpected irregularities in form. It begins by repeating bars 9–20 (12 bars) from the first part of the song. This repetition includes the second eight-bar period of Chorus 1 and the first four-bar phrase of the Bridge, a remarkable coalescence that associates, musically, the interrogative mode of line 9 of Chorus 1 with that of lines 18 and 19 of Chorus 2:

Line 9: "Who knows why an April breeze never remains?"
Line 18: "Is this what I've waited for?"
Line 19: "Am I the one?"

This wonderful remote juxtaposition of lyrics leaves the last two lines, 20 and 21, to be set by the final four bars of music—in effect a coda that leads to the final cadence on the tonic note in the melody in bar 20 and thus completes the rounded large-scale form of the song, which is summarized neatly as:

Chorus 1   16 bars
Bridge   16 bars
Chorus 2   16 bars

Of course this very regular display does not begin to indicate the special asymmetries and unexpected repetitions in the song that lend it its remarkable energy and vitality.

■

HAROLD ARLEN, "COME RAIN OR COME SHINE"
Lyrics by Johnny Mercer
CD Track 19

Ex. 4-18. "Come Rain Or Come Shine": Leadsheet

LYRICS
Refrain
Chorus I

1 I'm gonna love you
2 Like nobody's loved you,
3 Come rain or come shine.
4 High as a mountain
5 And deep as a river,
6 Come rain or come shine.

Bridge

7 I guess when you met me
8 It was just one of those things,
9 But don't ever bet me,
10 'Cause I'm gonna be true if you let me.

Chorus 2

11 You're gonna love me
12 Like nobody's loved me,
13 Come rain or come shine.
14 Happy together,
15 Unhappy together
16 And won't it be fine.
17 Days may be cloudy or sunny,
18 We're in or we're out of the money,
19 But I'm with you always,
20 I'm with you rain or shine!

The year in which *St. Louis Woman* was presented on Broadway was re-markable for the dynamic domestic and international events that took place in that first full year after the end of World War II. Winston Churchill coined the term "iron curtain" to describe the division between the Western nations and the U.S.S.R., which persisted until 1990. As one of many effects of that division Korea was split into northern and southern sectors, with Russia overseeing the north and the United States in charge of the south. The Nuremberg trials at-tempted to identify and punish those responsible for criminal acts during the war. At the trials, German Air Minister Hermann Goering committed suicide by taking a cyanide pill. The communists were trying to take over in China, and in the United States there was a huge and costly strike by coal miners.

Postwar attendance at musical events broke records, and in general, cultural life in the arts began to return to normal. In the popular arts, Irving Berlin's *Annie Get Your Gun* opened on May 14 and ran for 1,147 performances, one of the longest runs in Broadway history. The Academy Award for Best Picture was given to *The Best Years of Our Lives*, set in contemporary postwar America. This film, which touched a vast proportion of the population, won eight awards in all.

Popular songs continued to attract attention, among them Berlin's "They

Say It's Wonderful" (from the blockbuster show *Annie Get Your Gun*), Hoagy Carmichael's "Ole Buttermilk Sky," and Harold Arlen's "Come Rain Or Come Shine," our present subject. As a love song that celebrated fidelity and long-term love, "Come Rain Or Come Shine" had a special meaning for the postwar generation of Americans, many of whom had undergone separation from loved ones and suffered all the uncertainties of postwar adjustment that were brought on by the war. The song has retained its popularity, due in no small part to Frank Sinatra's 1961 recording.[15]

"Come Rain Or Come Shine" became the best-known song to appear in the Arlen-Mercer musical, *St. Louis Woman*, which featured an all-black cast.[16] The show opened March 30, 1946, and ran for just 113 performances. Although it was a commercial failure, the show contained a number of very fine songs, reflecting Arlen's continuing development as a songwriter, a process that was to bring him very close to the boundary between art songs and popular songs. Representative of this stage is "I Wonder What Became Of Me," which was dropped from the show but published in sheet music form. "Come Rain Or Come Shine" contains at least one feature that places it firmly within this transitional repertoire, and I will discuss that feature below.

Lyrics

In *St. Louis Woman*, "Come Rain Or Come Shine" was performed as a duet: "Della Green" (Pearl Bailey) sang Chorus 1 and the Bridge, while "Little Augie" (Rex Ingraham) sang Chorus 2. This dramatic situation may account for the character of the lyrics, the second part of which (Little Augie's) simply verifies and elaborates upon the first part. There is no dénouement, no twist at the end, with the exception of the unusual harmonic ending discussed below, which suggests various interpretations.

As lyrics, in the tradition of this genre, the text of "Come Rain Or Come Shine" is not outstanding. It contains three "gonnas," which many purists would regard as overuse of this colloquial American contraction, amply represented in political speeches of the Fourth of July variety. There are no inner rhymes and no remote rhymes, and the only word in the title phrase that is rhymed is "shine" (by "fine"). There are, incidentally, interesting references to two other songs in the repertoire. The first of these is heard in lines 4 and 5: "High as a mountain/And deep as a river," which paraphrases "How deep is the ocean/How high is the sky" from Irving Berlin's 1932 ballad, "How Deep Is The Ocean." The second and literal quotation is line 9 of the lyrics of "Come Rain Or Come Shine": "It was just one of those things," which is identical to the first line of the lyrics of the Refrain of Cole Porter's "Just One Of Those Things."[17]

Despite all these alleged defects, the lyrics work. Why? On the semantic side, they project a basic idea, a celebration of fidelity. As I suggested above, this is one of the main reasons the song became memorable and remains in the repertoire of classic American popular song. There are not many songs that deal so explicitly with this theme. On the sonic side, and at the very start of the song, it is Mercer's placement of the title phrase exactly at the end of the first and second melodic phrases in Chorus 1 (and at the end of the first phrase of Chorus 2) that is so effective (Ex. 4-19). Moreover, "shine" is made to shine by virtue of its duration—the longest of any word in the text.

The impact of the title phrase derives not only from its placement at the end of the melodic phrase but from the marked change in the melody precisely at those moments. It is at the ends of the melodic phrases that the declamatory pat-

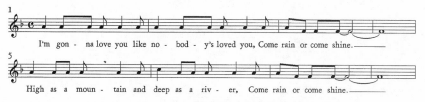

Ex. 4-19. *"Come Rain Or Come Shine": Opening music*

tern of repeated notes breaks and the melody drops down, expressively, for the lyric "rain or come shine" (Ex. 4-19).

Subsequent variants on this descending leap form a recurring motive throughout "Come Rain Or Come Shine."

Ex. 4-20 chronicles its occurrences in the song at crucial moments in the lyrics. After the original form of the motive in bars 4 and 8 (on A and F), the descending contour of "met me" in bar 10 (Ex. 4-20b) suggests a kindred form, one that is enlarged. The rhyming "bet me" in bar 14 (Ex. 4-20c) shrinks "met me" to a smaller size, closer to the original form. Bar 15 (Ex. 4-20d) begins on the notes of "bet me" (Eb-C), now setting the offensive "gonna," and continues sequentially on Bb and G, setting "if you." These forms of the motive, closely related by contour to the original form, are slightly smaller in terms of the interval between their two constituent notes—creating a "minor third," while the original form of the motive spans a "major third." At bar 23, however (Ex. 4-20e), the original interval of the motive, but not the original notes, sets "won't it be fine," delivering a distinctly optimistic message.

Ex. 4-20. "Come Rain Or Come Shine":
Important motive

The End of the Song and the "Two Key" Feature

However, the final form of the motive at the end of the song in bar 31 (Ex. 4-20f) sets "shine" in a harmonic context that invokes the blues, suggesting an ironic ending, or a sad ending, or an emotional incompleteness of some kind. Moreover, the final sonority in the song is not the usual tonic chord, which would be an F major chord, but a D major chord. Thus, the song may be heard to begin in one key (F) and end in another (D).[18] Not only that, but in the closing music the key of D has two aspects, major and minor: D major literally mixes with D minor. We hear this as the voice sings "shine" for the last time, as shown in Ex. 4-21.

While the voice sings a fragment of the D minor scale, the piano plays a sonority drawn from the D major scale, creating a complex sound, one that might be interpreted in the context of these lyrics as a musical emblem that combines "rain *and* shine."

The opposition of major and minor occurs elsewhere in "Come Rain Or

D major chord
(w/added 7th and 6th)

*Ex. 4-21. "Come Rain Or Come
Shine": Closing sonority*

Come Shine," notably in the Bridge, which changes the mode of the song to F minor, a change that is matched beautifully by the lyrics, "I guess when you met me/It was just one of those things." Thus, the contrast of major and minor pervades and unifies the entire song, creating the ABA'C succession of parts summarized below:

Form and key relations

A	bars 1–8	Lines 1–6	Key: F major
B (Bridge)	bars 9–16	Lines 7–10	Key: F minor
A'	bars 17–24	Lines 11–16	Key: F major
C	bars 25–32	Lines 17–20	Key: D major/D minor

Remarkably, the appearance of D minor and its companion, D major, at the end of "Come Rain Or Come Shine" is foreshadowed, and very audibly so, at strategic moments throughout the song, beginning with the first setting of the title phrase in bars 3 and 4 (Ex. 4-18) and again in bars 19 and 20 (Ex. 4-18). It is at this point that the D minor sonority is extended to set "Happy together." And from here to the end of the song the tonality gravitates away from F major and toward D major/D minor. We can now understand how meaningful is the dualism "rain" and "shine" in the title phrase of this song, reflected in the opposition of F major/F minor, D major/D minor, and, on the largest scale, by the opposition of the keys F and D.[19]

Pervading "Come Rain Or Come Shine" is the blues, a strictly American idiom that fascinated many American songwriters, notably Jerome Kern (*Show Boat*), George Gershwin (*Porgy and Bess*), and Harold Arlen (everywhere).

Melodic Highlights

Beyond the special issues of harmony in "Come Rain Or Come Shine," there remains much to be said about its melody, in addition to the prominent role of a single motive discussed above. Perhaps the most obvious feature of the melody is the repeated note (A) at the very beginning, which has attracted a lot of attention. There are thirteen repetitions in all (not an auspicious number). Mercer's declamatory lyrics are admirably suited to the repeated pattern, conveying the lover's insistence and determination.

To move now to the Bridge, the reader will easily recognize the essential ascending contour of the melodic line as it peaks on "bet" in bar 14 (Ex. 4-18), then descends rapidly from that same note on "gonna be true if you let me (Ex. 4-20d). But this peak note, Eb, is not the apex of the melody. The apex is reserved for the very end of the song; it is the high F that sets "shine!" in bar 31 (Ex. 4-18), a striking sonic symbol of the pervasive blues element in this song.

Of the other special melodic notes in "Come Rain Or Come Shine," the listener may respond strongly to the note that is repeated twelve times in bars 21–22, the first such repeated pattern after the repeated As. This note, B, is out of the key of F major, and unequivocally within the D minor orbit. In terms of the lyrics it takes on a special quality as it sets the dualistic text "Happy together, Unhappy together," foreshadowing the move to the D minor key. In the most extraordinary way, however, the appearance of the D major harmony at bar 25 on "Days may be cloudy or sunny" confounds our expectations. It also begins the ecstatic progression toward the climax of the song, the final setting of "shine" in bar 31, a progression that takes on a different and more intense coloration with the arrival on D minor at bar 29, setting "I'm with you always."

The harmonic dualism that is so prevalent in this song lends it a certain degree of ambivalence—intentional ambivalence, I feel, that relates to its musical theater context, but that has long since become a quality associated permanently with it.

■

JIMMY VAN HEUSEN, "BUT BEAUTIFUL"
Lyrics by Johnny Burke
(Not on CD)

LYRICS
Verse

Who can say what love is?
Does it start in the mind or the heart?
When I hear discussions on what love is,
Ev'rybody speaks a diff'rent part.

Ex. 4-22. "But Beautiful": Leadsheet

Refrain

A

Love is funny or it's sad,
Or it's quiet or it's mad.
It's a good thing or it's bad,
But beautiful!

B (Bridge)

Beautiful to take a chance,
And if you fall, you fall.
And I'm thinking,
I wouldn't mind at all.

A

Love is tearful or it's gay.
It's a problem or it's play.
It's a heartache either way,
But beautiful!

C

And I'm thinking if you were mine,
I'd never let you go.
And that would be
But beautiful, I know.

In 1947, the second year of relative peace following the end of World War II, India achieved independence from Britain, with the partitioning of the subcontinent into Hindu India and Moslem Pakistan. Dichotomies prevailed elsewhere. While George C. Marshall proposed the Marshall Plan to rebuild Western Europe, in the United States the House of Representatives' Un-American Activities Committee, responding to anti-communist anxieties, indicted ten Hollywood figures for contempt.

It was a big year for movies, with *Gentlemen's Agreement*, on the theme of concealed anti-Semitism, receiving the Motion Picture Academy's Award for Best Picture. On Broadway, *Finian's Rainbow* (Burton Lane and E. Y. Harburg) and *Brigadoon* (Alan Jay Lerner and Frederick Loewe) were major hits, with 725 and 581 performances, respectively, which reflected the public's current taste for folksy musicals. The death of Jerome Kern in 1946 had signaled the approaching end of the "golden era" of American popular song as it had developed since the twenties, and Jimmy Van Heusen was among the few major songwriters who made up the rear guard.

Jimmy Van Heusen and "But Beautiful"

Hollywood songwriter Jimmy Van Heusen (1913–1990) is the composer of "Imagination," "It Could Happen to You," "I Thought About You," and "The Second Time Around," among many other fine songs.[20] Like Harry Warren, Van Heusen's career as a songwriter was almost exclusively connected with the movies and with such figures as his personal friends Bing Crosby and Frank Sinatra.[21]

In a striking alliterative confluence, "But Beautiful" made its debut in the B-movie *Road to Rio*, starring Bob Hope and Bing Crosby, one of the "Road to" series of movies designed primarily as vehicles for their popular stars. In *Road to Rio*, Bing Crosby, replete with trademark bow tie, sings the song, very beautifully, to Dorothy Lamour, the glamorous female lead, clad in a slinky evening dress. As is often the case in these movie musicals, the song had virtually nothing to do with the plot, which was fortunate for the song. However, "But Beautiful," subsequently recorded by band leader Tex Beneke, shared the popularity of the movie to some extent, appearing on "Your Hit Parade" on February 14, 1948, where it stayed for nine weeks and rose to third place once, which was quite a record for a song that sophisticated.[22]

Lyrics

Johnny Burke, the highly regarded lyricist-songwriter, sometimes called "The Irish Poet," was closely associated with Bing Crosby, who sings "But Beautiful" in *Iceland*. The movie, which takes its name from its pseudo-authentic geographical setting, stars the virtuoso Norwegian ice skater Sonja Henie. The lyrics for the song exemplify Burke's considerable talent as well as his more modern approach to lyric writing, in which he used a combination of blank verse and rhymed verse. It is perhaps his most elegant production.

After the charming Verse (not sung in the movie), which sets the topic of the Refrain, the ever-popular *love*, we hear Burke's ingenious opening litany of that human behavioral oddity's characteristics, set out in three triple-rhyming lines. As soon becomes apparent, "threeness" is a primary feature of "But Beautiful," and I shall return to that topic below.[23] The rhyming triple of the first three lines, "sad, mad, bad," has its counterpart in the return of the A section (Ex. 4-22, beginning in bar 17), which presents the end-rhyme succession "gay, play, way." Remarkably, there is only one word in the lyrics that contains exactly three syllables, and that is the key word in the title, "beautiful," to which the three opening lines lead so beautifully.

Of the four unrhymed lines in the lyrics, the first is the alliterative title phrase "But Beautiful" itself. The sensitive word "beautiful" is always difficult to rhyme, and few lyricists have dared place it in such an exposed location, where it invites, but does not receive the rhyming word (if there is such) that might well have spoiled its effect.

Melodic and Rhythmic Motives

The beginning of the melody of the Refrain of "But Beautiful" exploits the "sequence," a type of melodic construction in which an initial figure provides a basic pattern that is then imitated by successive figures at higher or lower pitch levels.[24] In this instance, the three figures that make up the sequence correspond to the first, second, and third lines of the lyrics.

Ex. 4-23 shows the three thematic figures of the sequence as they slowly negotiate an ascending trajectory that arrives on the peak note D ("good thing")

Ex. 4-23. "But Beautiful": Sequence

in bar 5. Each figure unfolds the same rhythmic pattern and almost the same melodic pattern. That is, the second figure is the same as the first but transposed up a whole step. The third and last figure, however, is not an exact (transposed) replica of the first two since it has to adjust in order to remain in the scale of the tonic key.

Each of the figures is composed of two distinctive motives, and these are identified in Ex. 4-24. The first motive consists of an ascending leap that spans the interval of a fifth, beginning with the leap from D to A ("is fun-"). The second motive differs radically from the first, moving down by the smallest possible (chromatic) steps.

In addition to these spatial melodic motives, the thematic figures divide into two rhythmic motives that correspond to the lyrics, beginning with "Love is funny" and "or it's sad." Notice the special role of the two short notes on "Love

Ex. 4-24. "But Beautiful": Two motives

Ex. 4-25. "But Beautiful": Title lyric

is" and "or it's." These prepare the rhythmic setting of the key word "beautiful" in bar 7 at the end of the long sequence (Ex. 4-25). Now, however, the two-note group, which sets the first two syllables of "beautiful," is very audibly accentuated, due to its position on a strong beat in the bar. In this way, via the long sequence of three figures that precedes the distinctive setting of the title phrase, melody, rhythm, and lyrics combine to create an aesthetically intriguing and charming musical statement.

The torchy message of "But Beautiful" is of course evident throughout the song, but becomes most explicit in section C in bars 26–28 (Ex. 4-26), where

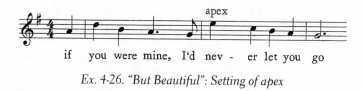

Ex. 4-26. "But Beautiful": Setting of apex

the lyrics match the melodic shapes perfectly, setting the only occurrence of the apex pitch E to highlight the syllable "nev-" in "never."

Verse

The Verse (Ex. 4-27), which consists of the traditional sixteen-bar double period, is set in the key of the dominant, D major, a somewhat unusual choice. Its relation to the music of the Refrain is surprisingly esoteric, and shows a side of

Ex. 4-27. "But Beautiful": Verse-Refrain connections

Van Heusen's songwriting skills that invites further study. Ex. 4-27 shows one of the several connections between Verse and Refrain. In the music at the end of the Refrain, Ex. 4-27a, we hear two descending leaps, the first a regular (perfect) fifth, the second a slightly smaller (diminished) fifth. These relate to the opening melody of the Refrain (Ex. 4-24) as contour reversals of the ascending leaps. In bars 3–4 of the Verse, shown in Ex. 4-27b, we hear the same intervals, and almost the same pitches, as the melody sets the rhetorical "Does it start in the mind." Here we have a remote textual relation combined with a very close musical connection, a phenomenon more often associated with classical music.

■

IRVING BERLIN, "STEPPIN' OUT WITH MY BABY"
Lyrics by Irving Berlin
CD Track II (with "Change Partners" and "Let Yourself Go")

Ex. 4-28. "Steppin' Out": Leadsheet

LYRICS
Refrain:
Chorus I
A (period)

1 Steppin' out with my baby.
2 Can't go wrong 'cause I'm in right.
3 It's for sure, not for maybe,
4 That I'm all dressed up tonight.

A (period)

5 Steppin' out with my honey,
6 Can't be bad to feel so good.
7 Never felt quite so sunny.
8 And I keep on knockin' wood, (There'll be)

B (Bridge)

9 Smooth sailin' 'cause I'm trimmin' my sails.
10 In my top hat and my white tie and my tails.

Chorus 2
A' (period)

11 Steppin' out with my baby
12 Can't go wrong 'cause I'm in right.
13 Ask me when will the day be,
14 The big day may be tonight.

The song "Easter Parade" was the big hit from the 1938 hit movie of the same name, which stars Fred Astaire and Judy Garland singin', dancin', and romancin'.[25] However, "Steppin' Out With My Baby," part of the Berlin medley on our compact disc, is featured in the last big production number in the movie. Astaire enters at the top of a set of stairs, in white suit, straw boater, and walking stick, sings "Steppin' Out With My Baby," then dances to five choruses of the song, played at different tempi, with four different girls, none of them Judy Garland or Ann Miller, but all of course fulfilling Hollywood requirements for plenteous pulchritude as well as terpsichorean talent.[26]

Lyrics

The key expression in the song's title, "Steppin' out," is somewhat dated slang. It means to dress up and (often) to spend money on an expensive outing, usually with a special person. In lines 8 through 9 "steppin'" generates a series of three participles with elided final g's: "knockin'," "sailin'," "trimmin'."[27] All four words celebrate this colloquial Americanism and form part of the cocksure mood of the lyrics that Astaire projects so convincingly in the movie scene, which, incidentally and perhaps not surprisingly, has nothing to do with the plot.[28]

The lyrics of both Chorus 1 and Chorus 2 are organized in rhyming couplets (*ab ab cd cd* for Chorus 1), while the two long lines (lines 9 and 10) of the eight-bar Bridge form a single couplet enhanced by the alliterations "smooth sailin'" and "tie," "tails." Another "incidentally": As indicated above, in the movie Astaire does not wear the formal dress described by "white tie" and "tails."

Lines 13 and 14 of the lyrics present the dénouement: "Ask me when will the day be/the big day may be tonight." Some readers may be intrigued by the phrase "the big day." Does this refer to engagement, to marriage, or to a transaction of a more transient nature?

Harmony

Going back to one of Berlin's most famous songs, "Blue Skies" (1927), for an example, the minor mode seems to have been a specialty of his, depicting a wide range of emotions. In "Steppin' Out With My Baby" it clearly supports the expression of masculine ego depicted by the lyrics, which verge on the "naughty." The main motive of the song is the ascending form of the D minor triad, shown in Ex. 4-29a. This motive occurs no fewer than six times in Chorus 1 alone. In addition, the reverse form of the triad, in descending contour, is heard twice, as shown in Ex. 4-29b, with the notes of the D minor triad filled in. The succes-

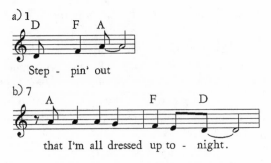

Ex. 4-29. *"Steppin' Out": D minor triad*

Ex. 4-30. "Steppin' Out": D major triad

sion D-F-A of the ascending form becomes A-F-D in the descending form that affirmatively closes each eight-bar period, emphasizing in that way the certainty conveyed by the megalomaniac lyrics.

After this strong presentation of the minor mode and the minor triad in particular, the strikingly exuberant change to the major mode for the Bridge of "Steppin' Out With My Baby" comes as a surprise. In the melody of the two almost identical four-bar phrases of the Bridge we hear an unfolding of the D major chord, the major counterpart of the D minor triad shown in Ex. 4-29a. Like the concluding phrase shown in Ex. 4-29b, the notes of this D major chord are not adjacent, but are stretched out over the entire phrase. Ex. 4-30 illustrates.

The juxtapositions of major and minor as well as other aspects of this music reflect the deep influence of the blues, to be found everywhere in Berlin's music.

Rhythm

Like all of Berlin's up-tempo movie songs "Steppin' Out With My Baby" is very syncopated. However, the syncopated phrases alternate with nonsyncopated music at strategic points, which frame the syncopated passages all the more effectively.[29] Thus, bars 1–6 of Chorus 1 repeat the same syncopated pattern four times. Bars 7–8, however, introduce a new rhythm that stresses the metrical pulse, specifically, on "I'm all dressed up to-."

At the beginning of the Bridge on the lyrics "smooth sailin'" and "I'm trimmin'," we hear a version of the traditional Charleston rhythm from the 1920s (see Ex. 1-21). The persistence of this micro-rhythmic figure over many years may be regarded as symbolic of the homogeneity of the classic American popular song repertoire, a beneficent uniformity that preserves common qualities and artistic strengths while allowing for the remarkable diversity we experience in the songs of the individual songwriters represented in this book. Indeed, it is this diversity that we most often celebrate, perhaps unconsciously, an attribute that allows us to associate the words "American" and "classic" in the special way so beautifully reified in the expressive join of music and words that we know as song.

CHAPTER FIVE

Conclusion

Now that we have completed our retrospective tour of the landscape of American popular song as its contours emerged during the quarter-century 1925–1950, it seems appropriate to offer a few words of conclusion—if, indeed, that word is at all appropriate in view of the very size of the repertoire, not to mention its diversity.

The idea of conclusion is even more suspect when we consider that this repertoire of popular song is still alive, still "popular." For this circumstance we have to thank not the entrepreneurs of mass media, but the professional musicians, the instrumentalists and singers, many of whose names are familiar to us, especially through recordings and movies. In the present age these artists, who regularly showcase popular songs from the golden era, work in a variety of fields: jazz, classical music (the so-called cross-overs), contemporary popular music, musical theater, cabaret, film music, television, radio and television commercials, even in rock. In short, this music remains a living part of our culture. Some people even regard it as America's "classical music."

In this connection I would venture a categorical statement: No other repertoire of fully notated music has undergone such remarkable transformations over such a long period of time, a process that continues today and one that the compact disc recordings in this volume amply exemplify. It is this process of constant renewal that keeps the repertoire alive and that distinguishes it from almost all of the concert repertoire that we cherish so.

At the beginning of this conclusion I referred to the size of the repertoire, a magnitude that could not be adequately represented in this book, with its concentration upon a select number of works. Nor was it possible to convey the extraordinary artistic diversity the songs exhibit, within the broadly conceived homogeneity that we have experienced in the melodic-rhythmic features, the formal paradigms, and, above all, in the harmonic language of these few beautiful songs. This brings me to yet another, but blessedly final categorical statement: taking into account the entire historical span of Western music, this repertoire of classic American popular song is distinguished by virtue of its status as the largest collection of homogeneous, fully notated, monophonic song with English language text.

Of all the characteristics that one might select to highlight as most distinctive of this music, it seems to me that the attributes of brevity, inextricably combined with intensity of musical and textual expression based upon a special language of melody, harmony, and rhythm that is uniquely American in character, are well qualified to set this repertoire apart from concert song repertoires traditionally associated with high culture. And of course I say this without in any way intending to disparage the wonderful classical song literature.

I would close by pointing out that because this repertoire of American popular song consists for the most part of music that is "simple," with lyrics intended to be accessible to a wide range of listeners who come to it from a variety of backgrounds and with various musical experiences, its expressive richness has not, by and large, been recognized at any level of detail. The best songs, and there are very many of them, are full of remarkable things. In the present volume, it has been the modest goal of the author and his colleagues Messrs. Lalli and Chapman to guide the reader toward a more satisfying listening experience, one that increasingly responds with greater sensitivity to the wonderful attributes of this music.

Notes

PREFACE

1. I have used the expression "around 1950," because some of the major figures continued to be productive past that date. I have in mind Cole Porter's *Can-Can* (1953), Harold Arlen's *House of Flowers* (1954), and the Rodgers & Hammerstein *Sound of Music* (1959)—although many would agree that that musical differs radically from the "classic" Rodgers & Hart songs of the golden period. With *Camelot* (1960), Lerner and Loewe penetrated even further into the next decade. However, the main vein of the golden era was almost exhausted by 1950, in terms of the number of songwriters producing major works, and, more important, the popular music scene was rapidly becoming dominated by rock 'n' roll, symbolized by the persona of Elvis Presley.

chapter one
PRELIMINARIES

1. The term *dominant* does not imply a power relation, but is the traditional term invented by the French music theorist Jean-Philippe Rameau in the early eighteenth century, for reasons known only to him. Together with the tonic, the dominant defines the key within which the scale resides. I remind the reader that all technical terms are defined in the "Glossary of Terms" as well as in the text proper.

2. Although "word painting" is discussed in the section on lyrics, the reader can easily guess what it refers to.

3. "Melodic coordinates" is a term introduced in Forte 1995.

4. For advanced readers, the details of motivic relations are more completely discussed in terms of the first three notes in the song, which form a unit that is repeated in inversion with "brown hair," in retrograde inversion with "zephyr on," and returns to the original form with "-yr on the."

5. I know that this definition of "tonality" is not especially informative to anyone who does not have a Ph.D. in music theory or musicology, but a better one would consume more space than is available in this modest volume—and also tax the author's resources.

6. Altered chords in the harmonic domain are analogous to the bending of meter by rhythm in the domain of rhythm. See the discussion on rhythm.

7. With respect to the classic American popular song repertoire, the actual historical origin of the chord of the added sixth is probably to be found in the pentatonic scale.

8. This aesthetic response probably derives from the minor triad with added sixth's association with the half-diminished seventh harmony. Compare the Cm6 in Ex.1–15a with the half-diminished seventh sonority in Ex.1–11d at 4.

9. It is not possible to generalize on "popular," since some contemporary popular songs involve single chords or a small number of chords that seem to be unrelated by the syntax of traditional tonal music.

10. This is sometimes also referred to as progression by "circle of fifths." I prefer "chain," since few progressions in these songs actually negotiate the entire circle of eleven fifths.

11. This song is discussed in Chapter 4.

12. For a recent study dealing with form see Caplin 1997.

13. Forte 1995, Chapter 6, provides a more detailed introduction to this topic.

14. Sometimes, however, the Verse is performed *after* the Refrain.

15. Of course there are exceptions. The Verse of the Rodgers and Hart song, "I Didn't Know What Time It Was" (Chapter 3) is 14 bars in length, and many verses have a tag of two bars that leads into the Refrain.

16. As far as I know, there is no published discussion of the criteria for a true Bridge in songs of the classic American popular song repertoire other than the brief treatment accorded that subject here.

17. The origin of the term *lyrics* (from which "lyricist" derives) to describe the text of a song is unknown to the author.

18. Exceptions to the music-first rule may be the songs of Cole Porter or those of Irving Berlin, where the songwriter and the lyricist are the same person.

19. The sheet music market is often synonymous with "Tin Pan Alley," often a mildly derogatory term.

20. The nature of meter and rhythm and their interaction has been the subject of theoretical discussion for many moons, and the brief treatment here is primarily for the purpose of preparing the reader for the nomenclature that will show up in the following chapters.

chapter two
SONGS FROM THE TWENTIES

1. Gershwin's *Rhapsody in Blue* was not, however, the first jazz-influenced orchestral composition. That was French composer Darius Milhaud's *La Création du monde*, 1923.

2. A contemporaneous recording of "Fascinating Rhythm" exists, on which Fred Astaire and his sister, Adele, sing to George Gershwin's piano accompaniment, with interspersed solos. From a synchronic perspective, this is the period of the "flapper," a wonderful time that looked ahead to the further emancipation of women in America.

3. See Steven E. Gilbert's study of the development of rhythm in Gershwin's music: Gilbert 1995, pp. 25–40. Gilbert also relates Zez Confrey's influence on Gershwin in

the area of rhythmic complexity (p. 32). Keller 1957 also has interesting comments on "Fascinating Rhythm," in the context of a comparison with Stravinsky's rhythmic usage.

4. The term syncopation comes from the Greek "syncope" applied to grammar, meaning a cutting short of what should be together.

5. Ex. 2–6 comes from the sheet music. Recorded performances may not preserve this regularity. Here the bass line strongly resembles a double bass figure.

6. Here I follow the arrangement of lines given by Ira Gershwin in Gershwin 1973, p. 103. The final punctuation mark there is the plaintive and interrogatory "?," not the expostulatory "!" that appears in the sheet music. It is at this point that the final and closing quotation mark also appears, to complete the rhetorical complaint of the singer.

7. The dates 1921 and 1923 are also given for the music of this show. I have taken the date 1925 for "Manhattan" from the opening of *Garrick Gaieties*, the show in which the song actually appeared. See Hyland 1998, p. 30.

8. Rodgers 1975, p. 65.

9. "How Long Has This Been Going On" was published in 1927, although it had been dropped from *Funny Face* after the tryout. In its reincarnation in *Rosalie* in 1928, it was reduced from a duet to a solo, sung by Rosalie. The sheet music, however, remains in the duet format. This has enabled the song to be sung by singers of either gender, which is especially advantageous in the Verse. See Kimball 1993, pp. 109–110, for the complete lyrics.

10. Gershwin 1973, p. 280.

11. Melodically, the final line is a stock blues figure — virtually identical to the one that sets "lovin' dat man of mine" in Jerome Kern's famous song, "Can't Help Lovin' Dat Man of Mine," from *Showboat*, which was composed in the same year, 1927.

12. For the history of the American popular song prior to the period with which this volume is concerned see Hamm 1979.

13. For harmonists I point out that the connection between this C major-seventh chord and a C flat-seventh blues-derived chord seems inescapable in the context of this song.

14. The tom-tom was often a musical symbol of the exotically erotic in the popular idiom of the era, especially in big band arrangements, where it was intended to arouse the dancers to ever greater terpsichorean heights. It shows up again in the Verse of Cole Porter's stunningly popular "Night and Day" from 1932.

15. In the Fifth Edition of *The Real Book* (the collection of "leadsheets" of songs that is used by many jazz groups), "What Is This Thing Called Love" appears, somewhat reharmonized, derived from Bill Evans's version on his album, "Portrait in Jazz." For readers with a background in harmony: Evans's opening chord of the Refrain is not Porter's dominant seventh on C, but a half-diminished seventh on C (II7 in F minor).

16. See "Glossary of Terms" for definitions of "major" and "minor."

17. A similar manipulation of this type of blue note (the "lowered third") at the ends of phrases was discussed in connection with Gershwin's song, "How Long Has This Been Going On?"

18. Not only is the blue note in the melody, but also the harmony is an F7 chord, or IV♭7, which is the first change in a standard blues progression. Although the F7 does not then behave as it would in a blues, the implication is momentarily in place.

19. According to Hischak 1995, p. 138, "I Guess I'll Have to Change My Plan" originated earlier as a song by Schwartz and Dietz that they wrote while working at a summer camp. It was entitled "I Love to Lie Awake in Bed"!

20. The progression that supports "gave her name as 'Missus'" is based upon a chain of fifths: A-D-G, ending on G major instead of the expected G minor. The G major, however, has a seventh attached to it, so that it serves as dominant, leading inexorably to the first chord of the Refrain, the C major triad. Some may wish to interpret the unexpected change at the end of the Verse as an instance of anacoluthon. I certainly could not object.

21. The term "mirror" is used quite loosely in writings on music. A true mirror image (reflection) of, say, the string of letters FBCD would reverse the string and each letter. This is known as "inversion." If the letters remain the same when reversed, the transformation (flipping over) is not noticeable. Thus, OMAHA becomes AHAMO. A true mirror image is therefore impossible to represent for a pitch string.

22. The reader may detect a certain uneasiness on the part of the author as he delivers these didactic messages. This is because he is uncertain of the extent to which the idioms of the day have been transmitted to the current generation.

chapter three
SONGS FROM THE THIRTIES

1. Gershwin dedicated his 1932 Songbook to Kay Swift, and her name is the source of the title of his musical, *Oh Kay!* (1926).

2. The Arthur Schwartz song "I Guess I'll Have To Change My Plans" in the present volume also comes from *The Little Show*, a revue for which Schwartz supplied virtually all the music.

3. To identify the references on the compact disc, Schmeling and Sharkey were boxing champions, German and American respectively. Amos and Andy were a beloved radio comedy team.

4. Perhaps some listeners will also detect the influence of Gershwin on the melodic-rhythmic patterns of the Refrain of "Fine and Dandy."

5. In the musical, the playboy character, Danny Churchill (Allen Kearns), and the prairie postmistress, Molly Gray (Ginger Rogers), express their mutual feelings of love by singing "Embraceable You."

6. The change to minor harmony and sometimes to minor key in the Bridge is very characteristic of Gershwin's songs. Two familiar instances: "The Man I Love" (1924) and "Nice Work if You Can Get It" (1937).

7. "Papa" follows logically from the idiomatic "baby." Presumably even grownup babies could have "papas" in those days.

8. Some singers actually sing E instead of E♭ at this point in the song.

9. In his widely read 1972 book, Alec Wilder refers to this scale degree as "the sixth interval," which is not a very accurate technical description.

10. Having written this categorical statement, I fully expect to receive counter-examples from irate readers.

11. It is easy to overlook the multiple functions of these songs. They were sung in the original context (musical theater, movies, big bands), appeared on the radio and on recordings, underwent live and recorded jazz interpretations, and (often overlooked nowadays) were danced to in the ubiquitous American ballrooms, especially during the Depression era.

12. Most verses, not only Gershwin's, were written after the Refrain, since the main idea of the song was contained in that music, and in the musical theater context—not so much in the movies—the Verse served a preparatory role in the advancement of the dramatic script.

13. In Forte 1995 I have discussed the connection of this passage to the Wagnerian "Tristan Chord."

14. Four-bar phrases of this kind appended to the standard sixteen-bar verse are sometimes called "vests," a term used sparingly in the present volume.

15. Among the famous performers who played at the Cotton Club were Duke Ellington and his Orchestra, Jimmy Lunceford's Orchestra, Cab Calloway, Ethel Waters, and a young Lena Horne, whose career began there. The floor shows were called "revues," a pseudo-French designation borrowed from Broadway and apparently intended to lend an air of refined entertainment.

16. In modern performances, the long-short ("dotted") rhythm is usually smoothed out to become an incomplete triplet: each pulse is divided into three durations, with the first note taking two of these, while the second note takes the remaining one. Sometimes these two-note figures are called "swing eighths" because the rhythmic figure is notated as two notes of equal value (eighth notes), and the performer supplies the idiomatic "swinging" rhythm by lengthening the first note of the pair.

17. Here and elsewhere I am aware that performers may not observe these notated distinctions with exactitude. Nevertheless, they exist conceptually with respect to the ideas of the songwriter and his lyricist.

18. As I indicated in note 10, Chapter 1, I prefer the term "chain of fifths" to describe this harmonic progression, since only rarely does such a progression actually traverse a complete "circle of fifths."

19. For those interested in the particulars of harmony, the shift here consists of a modulation to the key of Ab major, the minor mediant in the key of the song, F major.

20. For some reason, Duke does not use "glasses" here, the word that belongs to the idiom, "rose-colored glasses." According to Webster's, "chattels" refers to "an item of tangible movable or immovable property except real estate, freehold, and the things which are parcel of it." Good grief! Ira Gershwin sometimes used such language in his lyrics to poke fun at the upper classes. Such gestures were definitely part of the class distinctions that became especially prominent during the years of the Great Depression.

21. This chord is almost a "Tristan" chord. A change from D♭ to E♭ would effect the necessary transformation.

22. It would be interesting if one could refer to the influence of Cole Porter here, an influence evident elsewhere in Duke's songs. But Porter's Manhattan song, "Down in the Depths on the Ninetieth Floor," from *Red, Hot and Blue*, dates from 1936, two years after "Autumn In New York." The songs have the same theme: a love-hate relation with New York (Manhattan).

23. John Alden Carpenter's 1926 ballet/orchestral suite, *Skyscrapers*, comes to mind as a singular pictorial work that included specific musical delineations of the New York skyline. It is not impossible that Vladimir Dukelsky knew of this work.

24. "First nighting" refers to an opening of a Broadway musical, always a gala occasion, and one that would have meant something special to Vladimir Dukelsky in his Vernon Duke personification.

25. Again, a modulation to the minor mediant key, A♭.

26. The high E is the leading tone in the key of F minor, a note that is normally committed to ascending resolution on the tonic note, but that here falls back to the note from which it came, C.

27. "Autumn Leaves" by Joseph Kosma and Jacques Prevert and Harry Warren's "September In The Rain" come to mind as specimens of the genre that celebrates the emotional vibrations of the fall season.

28. "Your Hit Parade," sponsored by Lucky Strike cigarettes, began in 1935. The placement of a song title on the weekly list was determined by record sales, radio performances, performances by band leaders, and sheet music sales. It is also apparent, from reviewing the "hits," that the reputation of the performer who had recorded the song was a major factor in the ranking. Almost any song recorded by, for example, Bing Crosby, was a strong candidate for a place on the list.

29. Like many movie songs, "I've Got You Under My Skin" has no verse. The absence of a verse no doubt has to do with cinematic conventions concerned with timing, as well as with an audience whose constituency differed markedly from that of the standard Broadway musical, an audience that had little patience with the subtleties that the verse often projects in a musical theater context.

30. The Cole Porter Collection at Yale contains a number of song lyrics, carefully typed with a blue ribbon, suggesting that Porter may have completed the lyrics before composing the melodies. At least in Porter's case, these documents may offer a provisional response to the ancient question: Which came first, the words or the music?

31. The progression, however, is absolutely regular: the second form, on B♭, is a fourth above the first form, on F, and the third, on E♭, is a fourth above the second form. Here again is evidence, if any is needed, of Porter's very meticulous calculation of musical relations.

32. "Snazzy" is an adjective, widely used in the 1930s, to designate, with a high level of approval, something that was flashy, attractive, and novel. By the strict movie code of the time it was not possible to show two actors of opposite sexes in the same bed.

33. Despite certain external similarities, notably, the recurrent refrain represented by "c," this eight-line pattern is not to be confused with the eight-line *rondeau* so popular in thirteenth and fourteenth century France.

34. The alternative, or Boston, reading seems implausible: "timber," "limber," "marimber."

35. Some readers may want to change this note (on "Let") to B♭, by singing or playing it, just to experience the effect that remaining in the minor mode would have at this juncture in the song.

36. Unlike the songs of many of his contemporaries, those of Berlin are often fully notated to show the rhythmic patterns he wanted to be performed.

37. In assessing these ratings on "Your Hit Parade" one should bear in mind the really big hits. The all-time winner on "Your Hit Parade" was Irving Berlin's 1942 song, "White Christmas," recorded by Bing Crosby, which occupied first place for many weeks and is still heard over and over (and over) during the Christmas season.

38. In her career as a talented lyricist, it must be remembered that Dorothy Fields had many connections through her brother, Herbert Fields, who was an eminent producer and writer for musical theater, connections that enabled her to break through the male bastion. In 1946 Dorothy and her brother collaborated to write the book for Irving Berlin's smash hit, *Annie, Get Your Gun*.

39. Milton Babbitt has pointed out that Kern seems to have been quite insensitive to lyrics, and impatient with his lyricists. Fortunately, the lyricists were not impatient with the music or with the songwriter. Babbitt 1985.

40. For the information of students of harmony, the Bridge begins in the key of G♭, which is a tonicization of bIII in the tonic key of E♭, and a harmonic location that is usually associated with the parallel minor key.

41. Hamden, Connecticut just happens to be the hometown of the author, who lives within a stone's throw from the former Wilder residence.

42. Irving Berlin did not write the music for all of the Hollywood musicals starring Fred Astaire and Ginger Rogers. Jerome Kern did the music for *Roberta* (1935) and for *Swingtime* (1936). The latter movie is the source of "The Way You Look Tonight," included in the present book.

43. Among the many other examples of long-range stepwise contours in the songs included in the present volume, the reader may be interested in looking at Cole Porter's "I've Got You Under My Skin," discussed earlier. See also Forte 1993.

44. Not understanding the deeper level of meaning they project, critics have seemed perplexed by the unusual surface features of this song. One writes: "Its innovative harmonies and oddly constructed melodic line made one of those songs appreciated by sophisticated listeners." Hyland 1998, 122.

45. The first bar of the Verse, "Once I was young," replicates the contour of a prominent segment of the melody of the Refrain, "know what time it was." In terms of actual notes and in addition to contour, the first bar replicates the melody of bar 6 of the Refrain, "lovely time it was."

46. The confluence of a B♭ major seventh chord and melodic headnote A are more than reminiscent of Strayhorn's "Chelsea Bridge," one of his famous instrumental arrangements for the Ellington band.

47. If the tonal distance from the tonic B♭ is measured by fifth, the B7 chord of bars 21–22 is remote, while if measured by half-step it is as near as possible. Strayhorn (and Ellington) would have understood this seemingly contradictory circumstance very well, since the measurements underlie many kinds of progressions in the music they were familiar with and that they were composing and arranging at the time.

48. Line 6 of the Refrain, "And make it seem gay," is perhaps a not so concealed reference to Billy Strayhorn's sexual orientation, discussed in a sensitive and sympathetic way in Hadju 1996.

49. As examples of Strayhorn's composing and arranging under Ellington's auspices, perhaps the most familiar are: "Take The 'A' Train" (1941), by Strayhorn alone, "Satin Doll" (1953), and "Day Dream" (1941). "Something to Live For," however, dates from 1939 or perhaps earlier. Hadju discusses the credit issue evenhandedly, but points out that "Something to Live For" was part of the "Mad Hatters" repertoire, the jazz group that Strayhorn led before he came to Ellington. Hadju 1996, p. 83.

50. Schuller 1989, 47.

51. Ellington, on the other hand, was innovating early in the 1930s. Perhaps the most remarkable instance of this is his famous hit song, "Sophisticated Lady," from 1933, which originated as a number for the Ellington band and was later furnished with lyrics of dubious quality ["Dining with some man in a restaurant/Is that all you really want."].

chapter four
SONGS FROM THE FORTIES

1. Multitalented Vera Zorina later married famous choreographer George Balanchine. Her appearance in *Star Spangled Rhythm* was not among her most notable credits.

2. Glenn Miller's orchestra, formed in 1937, was one of the top bands during the war—up to his death in 1944, at which time he was leading an Army band. Its popularity no doubt contributed to the high ranking of "That Old Black Magic" on "Your Hit Parade."

3. The Academy Award for Best Picture of 1942 went to *Mrs. Miniver*, a study in high-class sentiment. Greer Garson was named Best Actress.

4. Jablonski 1961, p. 144. Among the lyricists of the American musical theater and motion pictures, Johnny Mercer belongs to the highest echelon. He wrote words for the melodies of many leading songwriters, including Hoagy Carmichael ("How Little We Know," which is on the CD in this volume), Jerome Kern ("I'm Old Fashioned"), Harry Warren ("Too Marvelous for Words").

5. Almost every performer today plays some variant on this sheet music figure.

6. For example, Harry Warren was only two years younger than Cole Porter.

7. In my opinion, the ratings on "Your Hit Parade" were very often influenced by the popularity of the groups or soloists who recorded the songs. For example, a recording by the Glenn Miller Orchestra was sure to attract the attention of the public.

8. The torch song exists in a number of variants. So common is the idiom that songs that include elements of the torch song are often referred to here as "torchy." In addition to "There Will Never Be Another You," torchy songs on the CD that accompanies this volume are Cole Porter's "What Is This Thing Called Love," his "Ev'ry Time We Say Goodbye," Arthur Schwartz's "I Guess I'll Have To Change My Plan," and Jimmy Van Heusen's "But Beautiful." As I indicated earlier, Harold Arlen's "The Man That Got Away," with lyrics by Ira Gershwin, sung by Judy Garland in the movie *A Star Is Born* (1954), may be taken as an authentic instance of the genre. See Glossary of Terms.

9. The first two descending contours of phrase 3 (B) are partial reversals (transposed) of the melody of A. While I doubt very much that Harry Warren thought of this relation in that way, he certainly intended to give phrase B maximally contrasting contours with respect to the preceding two phrases, and that is achieved by the process of reversal.

10. This alternation is clearly indicated in the chord symbols for each of the first three bars: "E♭" followed by "Cm." Unfortunately, this oscillating idea, which is so closely tied to the idea of parting and reconciliation basic to the song, is not consistently observed in recorded performances, even in such "authoritative" interpretations as Ella Fitzgerald's in "The Cole Porter Songbook."

11. Alec Wilder, who usually does not like repeated notes at all, refrains from negative comment on this instance, emphasizing, instead, the two-chord succession, which he also finds at the beginning of the 1940 Rodgers & Hart song, "It Never Entered My Mind." Wilder 1972, p. 247. Another famous instance is Harold Arlen's 1946 song, "Come Rain Or Come Shine," the opening melodic note of which is repeated thirteen times!

12. For the academically inclined cognoscenti I should point out that the chord Porter actually writes is a half-diminished seventh with F in the bass (Fm7♭5), which of course contains an A♭ minor triad, and thus gives the effect of a "change from major to minor."

13. Even though his role in the movie was minor, Hoagy Carmichael was no doubt also a drawing card. His movie career, in which he played himself, established him as a genuine American folk figure, somewhat like the later Burl Ives. The only other songwriter of the era to attain extensive public visibility was George Gershwin, whose flamboyant personality was always of interest. Irving Berlin occasionally surfaced from his estate in Fisher's Eddy, and appeared in the movie, for which he wrote the music, *This Is The Army (Mr. Jones)*.

14. The history of the Latin influence upon American popular song is complex, since it involves a second level of the fusion of African and European music separate from American jazz, which was one of the conduits for the transmission of Latin rhythms to popular song and very likely the source of Hoagy Carmichael's rhythmic patterns in "How Little We Know." By 1944 Latin rhythms were well established in American popular music, having first entered in the 1920s.

15. Sinatra also included a new recording of this song on his Duets (1993).

16. This was not the only similarity between *St. Louis Woman* and Gershwin's *Porgy and Bess.*

17. From *Jubilee* (1935). The song became popular only in the 1940s, and was current in 1946. Of course "just one of those things" is a colloquial phrase and therefore in public domain.

18. Non-tonic endings are sometimes found in nineteenth-century art songs, for example, in the songs of Hugo Wolf. Writers sometimes comment on this apparent aberration, but usually do not offer an interpretation. Hischak writes: "Arlen's music [for "Come Rain Or Come Shine"] is unusual in that it has no verse and starts in one key only to end in another." Hischak 1995, p. 55. Wilder 1972 does not mention this feature at all. For an effort to explain the anomaly see Forte 1995, p. 230.

19. Of course Johnny Mercer probably did not see these relations in the systematic way I have presented them here. But certainly when he first heard the music he perceived at least some of the "rain-shine" contrasts in terms of the juxtapositions of harmonies and keys.

20. Jimmy Van Heusen's real name was Edward Chester Babcock. He derived his professional name from the label on a shirt collar.

21. Exceptions are the well-known songs "Darn That Dream" (1939) and "Here's That Rainy Day," both written for Broadway musicals.

22. As usual, the qualities of "But Beautiful" were apparently not fully appreciated by the public. On the February 14, 1948 broadcast of "Your Hit Parade," the number one slot was taken by "Ballerina," a song that has long since vanished.

23. Another song that features "threeness," one perhaps more famous than "But Beautiful," is the Rodgers and Hart song, "Bewitched."

24. Musicians who study and perform classical music sometimes look down on the sequence, regarding it as a vulgarization of melody. In "But Beautiful" the combination of the opening formulaic sequence with the striking and unexpected culmination in the special rhythm and rich harmony of bar 7 that set "beautiful" illustrates the juxtaposing of the mundane and the extraordinary that is frequently apparent in the best of the American popular songs, in Gershwin's, for example. And the motivic content of the sequence itself, which leads, inexorably, to the setting of "beautiful," removes the melody from the lowly category of the cliché.

25. "Easter Parade" was on "Your Hit Parade" for ten weeks. "Steppin' Out With My Baby," however, did not appear.

26. Ann Miller, virtuoso tap dancer, had been a partner of Fred Astaire, but was given only second billing in *Easter Parade*, yielding to America's sweetheart, Judy Garland.

27. "Knockin' wood," as I'm sure many readers know, is short for "knock on wood," a superstitious gesture intended to assure safe continuation of the condition being described.

28. Overlaid on the flimsy plot of *Easter Parade* is a reincarnation of the Broadway revue, a series of musical acts featuring the stars, often with spectacular Hollywood sets and

full orchestra accompaniment, occasionally augmented by vocal chorus, with, of course, ever-present chorus girls and boys.

29. Berlin's syncopated rhythms must have been carefully notated by his "musical secretary." The piano part in the sheet music is professional to the last dotted quarter note. The practice of many other songwriters was to notate straight, unsyncopated rhythms, leaving the jazzy interpretations to the performer. The sheet music then looked less complicated and less forbidding to the amateur pianists who were likely to purchase it.

Glossary of Terms

Terms in italics are defined in separate entries in the Glossary.

Alliteration. The repetition of a beginning consonant sound for a series of two or more words.

Anacoluthon. "The passing from one construction to another before the former is completed." The Oxford English Dictionary.

Apex. The highest melodic note in the melody. Compare with *nadir*.

Aposiopesis. A rhetorical artifice in which the speaker comes to a sudden halt, as if unable or unwilling to proceed (The Oxford English Dictionary).

Augmented Triad. A major triad with raised (augmented) fifth degree. An example is C-E-G♯.

Blank verse. Verse with meter (e.g., *iambic*), but without rhyme.

Bar. A unit of measurement that segments the music notationally. Synonymous with measure. A notational unit circumscribed by vertical lines known as bar lines.

Barform. An ancient form consisting of statement-statement-response, or AAB. The twelve-bar blues is an example, and there are many examples in classical concert music, for instance, in Wagner's opera, *Die Meistersinger von Nüremberg*.

Bar line. The notational symbol, a vertical line that traverses the five lines of the staff, delimiting the *bar*.

Blue notes. These are often described as altered notes in the prevailing scale or key of a piece: the lowered diatonic third and seventh degrees and the lowered fifth in major, the lowered fifth in minor.

Bridge. The second and contrasting section in many songs in the classic American popular song repertoire.

Cadence. A harmonic and melodic formation that ends a phrase.

Charleston. A popular ballroom dance style of the 1920s and later. The Charleston rhythm, which pervades many popular songs of the era, is a two-pulse syncopation notated as dotted quarter followed by eighth note tied to half note. Its origins are to be found in Latin American patterns.

Chord symbols. The system of shorthand used on *leadsheets* to tell the performer/reader what notes make up a chord.

Chorus 1. In a Refrain, the section of an ABA song form that precedes the Bridge.

Chorus 2. In a Refrain, the section of an ABA song form that follows the Bridge, repeating, perhaps with some variation, Chorus 1.

Chromatic. Notes that lie outside the tonic or keynote scale. In the key of E♭, the note F♭ is a chromatic note.

Chromatic alteration. The lowering or (especially) the raising of a *diatonic* note by one half-step. For example, in the key of C, F♯ may be regarded as a chromatically altered version of the diatonic note F, scale degree 4.

Consonant. Relatively uncommitted with respect to motion. Not required to move in a particular way. Stasis.

Contour. The shape of a melody determined by the upward and downward path it describes.

Contrasting period. A *period* the constituent melodic phrases of which are dissimilar.

Decoration. A note, usually of short duration, that decorates another, more important note.

Diatonic. Notes of the natural scale defined by the key signature.

Diminished triad. A triad consisting of an arrangement of minor thirds, beginning from the lowest note. An example is C-E♭-G♭.

Dissonant. Usually dependent upon a real or implied motion to a consonance. Dynamic in effect, producing motion. *Cf. Consonant*

Dominant. The note or *scale degree* that lies a fifth above the tonic note.

Double period. Two periods in succession. See *Period*.

Downbeat. The first metrical pulse in a bar. See *Meter*.

Duration. The time occupied by a note, symbolized in music notation by various note shapes, such as the quarter note or the half note.

Dynamics. The relative loudness of a note, melodic configuration, harmony, passage, etc.

End rhymes. Rhymes located at the ends of lines, as distinct from *inner rhymes*.

Enharmonic. The variable notational spelling of a pitch. For example, the pitch that sounds as middle C can also be notated as B♯ or D♭♭.

Form. The succession of parts of a song.

Half step. The distance or *interval* from one note of the scale to another with no note in between. For example, the space from E to F in the C major scale is a half step. Also: The smallest distance from one note to another. For example, from middle C on the keyboard to the black key immediately to the right of it (D♭) or to the white key immediately to the left of it (B).

Harmonic progression. A succession of chords.

Headnote. The first note in a melody or a melodic configuration.

Inner rhyme. Word pairs in which internal syllables rhyme, providing a special sonic connection—as "string" and "finger," or rhyming word pairs within the line, as distinct from *end rhymes*.

Inner rhymes. The situation in which rhyming words occur within lines, in addition to or instead of at the ends of lines.

Internal rhymes. The situation in which syllables within words rhyme.

Interval. The distance from one note to another, measured by the number of diatonic notes traversed, beginning with the first note. With reference to the C scale, the interval from C up to G is a fifth since it spans five diatonic notes: C-D-E-F-G.

Key. In music notation, this refers to the sharps or flats (or neither) that follow the clef sign. Thus, three flats designate the key of E♭ major or C minor.

Keynote. See *Tonic*.

Leadsheet. An abbreviated form of notation often used for popular songs. It consists of the melodic line alone, with chord symbols. In the present book, lyrics are included in the leadsheet.

Lyrics. The words of a song.

Major. For our purposes, the distinction between major and minor thirds is important. The minor third spans an interval of three half steps, as from C to E♭. The major third spans an interval of four half steps. Also applies to chord qualities. A minor chord (triad) consists of three notes, the lower two of which form a minor third. The lower two notes of a major triad form a major third. See also *Minor*.

Major scale. The series of seven notes, usually displayed in ascending order, comprising the series of *intervals* whole step-whole step-half-step-whole step-whole step-whole step-half step.

Major Triad. A three-note chord (triad) consisting, from the lowest note upward, of a major third surmounted by a minor third. C-E-G is an example. See *Major*.

Melodic coordinate. A special note in a song, such as the apex or highest note.

Meter. The system of regular pulses in a song. Most songs of this era are in what is called *alla breve* meter or "cut time": Each bar of music is divided into two pulses, the first of which is accented.

Meter signature. The notated symbol that gives the performer basic information about the *meter* of the song. The signature 3/4 indicates that each bar will contain 3 quarter notes (the numeral 4) or their equivalent.

Minor. A key, harmony, or scale that is often characterized as "sad," "tragic," "foreboding," and so on. It contrasts, traditionally, with the brighter sounding *major* tonality or major harmony. Chopin's famous Funeral March is, aptly enough, in a minor key. Like all definitions, this one is subject to exceptions. In the present volume, Irving Berlin's "Steppin' Out With My Baby" is a very sanguine song in a minor key (except for the Bridge).

Minor triad. A three-note chord (triad) consisting, from the lowest note upward, of a minor third surmounted by a major third. C-E♭-G is an example. See *Minor*.

Motive. Usually a short melodic fragment that is repeated sufficiently often to attain an identity.

Nadir. The lowest melodic note in the melody. Compare with *Apex*.

Octave. A distance of eight diatonic notes. Notes related at this distance, *mutatis mutandis*, are often considered replicas. Octave-related notes bear the same letter-name.

Ostinato. An obstinate melodic figure in the bass that is repeated over and over and over, as in Ravel's *Bolero*.

Parallel period. A *period* the constituent melodic phrases of which are similar.

Pentatonic scale. A five-note scale. A model for this scale consists of the group of five black keys on the piano, or the first five white keys beginning on middle C and skipping the fourth key (F).

Period. Two consecutive phrases, each four bars in length. Two four-bar melodic units.

Phrase. A musical unit defined by an onset and a closure (cadence). In the repertoire of classic American popular song, the phrase is usually four bars in length. Usually a four-bar melodic unit.

Refrain. The main part of the song, following the Verse (if any).

Register. The spatial location of a note, melody, or chord. Middle C on the piano is in the middle register, while Cello C is in the lower register.

Release. Another term for Bridge, which is also sometimes called "the middle eight."

Remote rhymes. Rhyming words that are located at a distance from each other in the lyrics and whose placement does not necessarily follow the rhyme scheme.

Rhythm. The durational and accentual pattern created by a melody or chord succession.

Scale degree. A note in the ordinary seven-note scale, arranged numerically from the lowest note, which is designated scale degree 1 (Do).

Semantic. Refers to the meaning of the lyrics, as distinct from their sound. The "meaning" of a word or *lyrics*. See *Sonic*.

Sequence. A series of melodic figures in which those that follow the first one replicate it at successively higher or lower pitch levels.

Sonic. Refers to the sound of the lyrics and their individual words, an important feature for musical settings. The sound of a melody or harmony, apart from any meaning that may be attached to it by virtue of the *lyrics*.

Syncopation. A pattern created by a melody or harmonic progression that disrupts the normal pattern of durations specified by the meter signature. Typically, a note or chord comes in before the metrical pulse to which it would belong were the rhythm made to conform to the meter (regularized).

Tailnote. The last note in a melodic configuration.

Tempo. The speed of a song, indicated by such terms as Allegro (fast), Adagio (slow).

Tonality. The large-scale abstract system of harmony that governs the structure of a particular song. Loosely construed, the *key* of a song.

Tonic. The main note in a *key*, which has the same name as the key. Eb is the keynote or tonic in the key of Eb. Whatever may be its diverse roles in the melody, the keynote is very often the final note in the song.

Torch song. The term "torch" derives from the idiom "to carry the torch" (for someone). The lyrics of the torch song reflect the emotional situation in which the singer finds himself or herself (generally the latter) from one-sided (unrequited) love symbolized by the "torch." In the extreme case, Individual A desperately loves Individual B, but Individual B is oblivious of the existence of Individual A or has loved but then abandoned Individual A, who expresses feelings of loss and deplores the behavior of Individual B, but nevertheless would welcome the return of Individual B to the love relationship under virtually any circumstances. In the American popular song idiom, appropriately enough, the music of the torch song generally contains melodic elements of the blues.

Transposition, transposed. The shifting of a melodic or harmonic configuration to another pitch level so that the distance between the notes of the new configuration (its intervals) remains the same. One also speaks of transposing to another key, as from Eb to F, which changes the pitch level by one whole step.

Tritone. A special relation (interval) between two notes that spans six semitones. In the melodic language of this repertoire, it may have ironic connotations, especially in connection with a descending contour, or deeply expressive, often amorous, implications.

Upbeat. A note or notes that precede the first metrical pulse in a bar. See *Downbeat*.

Verse. The introductory section of a song, normally sixteen bars in length.

Whole step. The distance or *interval* from one note of the scale to another with one note in between. For example, the space from C to D in the C major scale is a whole step because there is one note in between the two notes: a C♯ or a D♭.

Word painting. A pictorial correspondence or symbolic correspondence of the semantic content of a section of the lyrics and the musical configuration(s) with which they are associated.

Bibliography

Armitage, Merle, ed. 1938. *George Gershwin*. New York: Longmans, Green & Co.

Babbitt, Milton. 1985. "All the Things They Are: Comments on Kern." *Institute for Studies in American Music Newsletter* 14: 8–9.

Barrett, Mary Ellin. 1994. *Irving Berlin: A Daughter's Memoir*. New York: Simon & Schuster.

Bergreen, Laurence. 1990. *As Thousands Cheer: The Life of Irving Berlin*. New York: Viking Penguin.

Campbell, Michael. 1996. *And the Beat Goes On: An Introduction to Popular Music in America, 1840 to Today*. New York: Schirmer Books.

Caplin, William. 1997. *Classical Form: A Theory of Formal Functions for the Instrumental Music of Haydn, Mozart, and Beethoven*. New York: Oxford University Press.

Forte, Allen. 1993. "Secrets of Melody: Line and Design in the Music of Cole Porter." *Musical Quarterly* 77: 607–47.

Forte, Allen. 1995. *The American Popular Ballad of the Golden Era, 1924–1950*. Princeton: Princeton University Press.

Forte, Allen. 1999. "Harmonic Relations: American Popular Harmonies (1925–1950) and Their European Kin." *Contemporary Music Review* 19: 5–36.

Gershwin, Ira. 1973. *Lyrics on Several Occasions*. New York: The Viking Press.

Gilbert, Steven. 1995. *The Music of Gershwin*. New Haven and London: Yale University Press.

Gordon, Lois and Alan, eds. 1995. *The Columbia Chronicles of American Life, 1910–1992*. New York: Columbia University Press.

Hadju, David. 1996. *Lush Life: A Biography of Billy Strayhorn*. New York: Farrar, Straus, Giroux.

Hamm, Charles. 1979. *Yesterdays: Popular Song in America*. New York: W. W. Norton.

Hamm, Charles. 1997. *Irving Berlin: Songs from the Melting Pot: The Formative Years, 1907–1914*. New York: Oxford University Press.

Hischak, Thomas. 1995. *The American Musical Theatre Song Encyclopedia*. Westport: Greenwood Press.

Hyland, William G. 1998. *Richard Rodgers*. New Haven and London: Yale University Press.

Jablonski, Edward. 1961. *Harold Arlen: Happy with the Blues*. New York: Doubleday.

Jablonski, Edward. 1987. *Gershwin*. New York: Doubleday.

Keller, Hans. 1957. "Rhythm: Gershwin and Stravinsky." *The Score and I.M.A. Magazine* 20: June 1957: 19–31.

Kimball, Robert, ed. 1992. *The Complete Lyrics of Cole Porter*. New York: Da Capo Press.

Kimball, Robert, ed. 1993. *The Complete Lyrics of Ira Gershwin*. New York: Alfred A. Knopf.

Peyser, Joan. 1993. *The Memory of All That: The Life of George Gershwin*. New York: Simon & Schuster.

Rodgers, Richard. 1975. *Musical Stages: An Autobiography*. New York: Random House.

Rosenberg, Deena. 1993. *Fascinating Rhythm: The Collaboration of George and Ira Gershwin*. New York: Penguin Books

Schuller, Gunther. 1989. *The Swing Era*. New York: Oxford University Press.

Sears, Ann, ed. 2001. *'S Marvelous! Wonderful! Studies of American Popular Song*. Westport: Greenwood Press.

Suskin, Steven. 1992. *Show Tunes, 1905–1991*. New York: Limelight Editions.

Wilder, Alec. 1972. *American Popular Song: The Great Innovators, 1900–1950*. Oxford: Oxford University Press.

Index

Music Credits

The Way You Look Tonight, Words by Dorothy Fields. Music by Jerome Kern. Copyright © 1936 by PolyGram International Publishing, Inc., and Aldi Music. Copyright Renewed. All Rights for Aldi Music Administered by the Songwriters Guild of America. International Copyright Secured All Rights Reserved.

MUSIC SALES CORPORATION

But Beautiful, Lyrics by Johnny Burke. Music by Jimmy Van Heusen. Copyright © 1947 (Renewed) by Onyx Music Corporation (ASCAP) and Bourne Co. All rights to Onyx Music Corporation administered by Music Sales Corporation (ASCAP). International Copyright Secured. All Rights Reserved. Reprinted by Permission.

WARNER/CHAPPELL MUSIC INC.

All rights to the following songs controlled and administered by Warner/Chappell Music, Inc. Copyright acknowledgment information pending. All rights reserved. Used by permission.

> Fascinating Rhythm (1924) Gershwin/Gershwin
> How Long Has This Been Going On? (1927) Gershwin/Gershwin
> Embraceable You (1930) Gershwin/Gershwin
> What Is This Thing Called Love? (1929) Porter
> I Guess I'll Have To Change My Plan (1929) Dietz/Schwartz
> I've Got The World On A String (1932) Koehler/Arlen
> I Didn't Know What Time It Was (1939) Hart/Rogers
> How Little We Know (1944) Mercer/Carmichael
> Fine and Dandy (1930) James/Swift
> Something To Live For (1939) Ellington/Strayhorn
> Autumn In New York (1934) Duke
> Come Rain Or Come Shine (1946) Mercer/Arlen

WARNER BROS. PUBLICATIONS INC.

AUTUMN IN NEW YORK, by Vernon Duke. © 1934 (Renewed) Warner Bros. Inc. All Rights Reserved. Used by Permission. WARNER BROS. PUBLICATIONS U.S. INC., Miami, FL 33014.

COME RAIN OR COME SHINE, Music by Harold Arlen, Words by Johnny Mercer. © 1946 (Renewed) Chappell & Co. All Rights Reserved. Used by Permission. WARNER BROS. PUBLICATIONS U.S. INC., Miami, FL 33014.